Language Arts Guide

Level 6

Siegfried Engelmann
Jean Osborn
Steve Osborn
Leslie Zoref

A Division of The McGraw-Hill Companies

Columbus, Ohio

Illustration Credits
Kate Flanagan

www.sra4kids.com

SRA/McGraw-Hill

A Division of The **McGraw·Hill** *Companies*

Send all inquiries to:
SRA/McGraw-Hill
8787 Orion Place
Columbus, OH 43240-4027

Printed in the United States of America.

ISBN 0-07-572385-9

1 2 3 4 5 6 7 8 9 DBH 06 05 04 03 02 01

Gift

Scope and Sequence for the *Language Arts Guide*

BOOK PARTS: TABLE OF CONTENTS

> **1**
>
> Name _____
>
> **Lesson 1**
>
> **A.**
>
> | Table of Contents | | |
> |---|---|---|
> | Lesson | Selection | Page |
> | 1 | A Trip through Time | 2 |
> | 2 | The Golden Fleece | 12 |
> | 3 | Sally and the Salamander | 16 |
> | 4 | The Magic Lantern | 22 |
> | 5 | Grandfather's Story | 38 |
> | 6 | The View from Mars | 50 |
> | 7 | Stars and Planets | 62 |
> | 8 | A New Home for Jessie | 86 |
>
> **B. Write the answer to each question.**
>
> 1. What part of a book shows a list of the selections in the book?
>
> _____
>
> 2. What is the title of the selection for lesson 3?
>
> _____
>
> 3. On what page does the selection for lesson 3 begin?
>
> _____
>
> 4. What is the title of the selection for lesson 7?
>
> _____
>
> 5. On what page does that selection begin?
>
> _____
>
> 6. What is the name of the selection that begins on page 22?
>
> _____
>
> 146   BLM 1

1. (Hold up a textbook and show the table of contents page.) This part of the book is called the **table of contents.**
- The table of contents is a list of the selections that are in a book.
- The order of the list of selections is based on the page number.
2. Find part A on your worksheet for lesson 1. ✔
3. The box shows a sample of a table of contents for a book. The first title on the list shows the selection that starts on page 2 in the book. The next title on the list shows the next selection in the book and the page number on which that selection begins.

- What is the title of the first selection in this book? (Idea: *A Trip Through Time*.)
- On what page does that selection begin? (Idea: *Two*.)
4. Read the title of the next selection in this book. (Idea: *The Golden Fleece*.)
- On what page does that selection begin? (Idea: *Twelve*.)
5. Just before the selection titles are lesson numbers. What's the title of the selection for lesson 5? (Idea: *Grandfather's Story*.)
6. Everybody, what's the selection for lesson 8? (Signal.) *A New Home for Jessie.*
- Everybody, on what page does that selection begin? (Signal.) *Forty-four.*
7. Find part B on your worksheet. ✔
- These are questions about some of the things we just went over. Follow along as I read item 1: **What part of a book shows a list of the selections in the book?** Everybody, what's the answer? (Signal.) *Table of contents.*
8. It's your turn. Write the answers to the questions on your worksheet.
9. (After students complete the items, do a workcheck. Read each item, then call on a student to answer it. If the answer is wrong, give the correct answer.)

Answer Key: 1. table of contents **2.** *Sally and the Salamander* **3.** 16 **4.** *Stars and Planets* **5.** 62 **6.** *The Magic Lantern*

Lesson 2

BOOK PARTS: INDEX

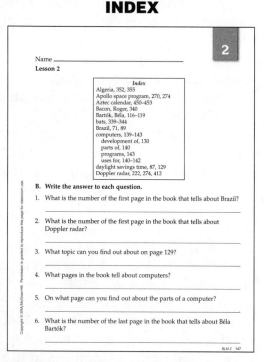

1. Look at your worksheet for lesson 2. ✔
2. The box shows one page of the part of a book that is called the **index.**
- The index lists the different topics in a book. The topics are listed alphabetically. The first topic in this index is **Algeria.** Touch that topic.
- The index shows the number of a page in the book that tells about Algeria. What page in this book tells about Algeria? (Idea: *352.*)
- Everybody, is that the only page that tells about Algeria? (Signal.) *No.*
- What's the other page in this book that tells about Algeria? (Idea: *355.*)

3. (Write on the board:)

> **280–301**

- Sometimes, a topic in the book takes up more than one page.
- (Touch the dash between the numbers.) If the numbers have a dash between them, they tell about a topic that takes up more than one page.
- If the index showed the numbers on the board for a topic, the numbers would tell you that the topic starts on page 280 and it continues until page 301.
4. Look at the page numbers in the index on your worksheet. Find the first place that shows a pair of numbers for a topic that takes up more than one page. Raise your hand when you've found it. (Observe students and give feedback.)
5. What is the name of the first topic that takes up more than one page? (Idea: *Aztec calendar.*)
- On what page does that topic start? (Idea: *450.*)
- On what page does that topic end? (Idea: *453.*)
6. It's your turn. Write the answers to the questions.
7. (After the students complete the items, do a workcheck. Read each item, then call on a student to answer it. If the answer is wrong, give the correct answer.)

Answer Key: 1. 71 **2.** 222 **3.** daylight savings time **4.** 139–143 **5.** 140 **6.** 119

BOOK PARTS: GLOSSARY

3

Lesson 3

Name _____

A.

famished		gallant

f

famished When you are *famished*, you are very, very hungry.
fat People used to use *fat* to fry food. Today, most people use cooking oil instead of fat.
fawn A *fawn* is a young deer.
feeble Something that is very weak is *feeble*.
fit When somebody has a *fit*, that person loses consciousness and may writhe around.
flask A *flask* is a king of bottle.
flee When you *flee*, you move as fast as you can.
fleece The fur of a sheep is called, *fleece*.
flinch When you *flinch*, you jump when somebody startles you.

fret When you worry about something, you *fret* about that thing.
frivolous Someone who is foolish and not serious is *frivolous*.
fulfill When something is *fulfilled*, that thing comes true.
furnish When you supply something, you *furnish* it.

g

gadget Another word for a *device* is a *gadget*.
gale A *gale* is a terrible storm with great winds.
gallant Somebody who is very brave and noble is *gallant*.

B. Look at the guide words for each page. Write the page number for each word.

page 171	gratify	inlet
page 172	insecure	jamboree
page 173	jealousy	lurk

1. intricate _____
2. lobby _____
3. hobble _____
4. isolate _____
5. kettle _____
6. jostle _____
7. idle _____

148 BLM 3

1. Find part A on your worksheet for lesson 3. ✔
2. The box shows a page from the part of the book called the **glossary.** A glossary gives the definitions, or meanings, of words used in the book.
   - The words in a glossary are in alphabetical order.
   - The two words at the top of the page are called **guide words.** The guide word on the left side tells you the first word defined on the page. The guide word on the right side tells you the last word defined on the page.
3. The guide word on the left side is **famished.** Touch that guide word.
   - That guide word tells you that the first word defined on the page is **famished.**

   - Touch the guide word on the right side. What's the guide word on the right side? (Idea: *Gallant.*)
   - That tells you that **gallant** is the last word defined on the page.
4. (Write on the board:)

diameter	exquisite

   - What's the first guide word? (Signal.) *Diameter.*
   - So what's the first word on the page? (Signal.) *Diameter.*
   - What's the second guide word? (Signal.) *Exquisite.*
   - So what's the last word on that page? (Signal.) *Exquisite.*
5. It's your turn. Look at part B. The words in the boxes are guide words for pages in a glossary.
   - Each word in the list goes on one of the glossary pages. After each word, write the page number on which you would find the word in a glossary. Raise your hand when you're finished. (Observe students and give feedback.)
6. (Write on the board:)

1. intricate	page 172
2. lobby	page 173
3. hobble	page 171
4. isolate	page 172
5. kettle	page 173
6. jostle	page 173
7. idle	page 171

7. Check your work. Here's what you should have. Correct any mistakes.

Lesson 4

Materials: Each student will need a copy of the worksheet for lesson 4 (Blackline Master 4).

BOOK PARTS:

Name _____

Lesson 4

For each item, write the name of the part of the book that you would use. The answer to each item is **table of contents, index,** or **glossary.**

1. You want to find out what reading selection starts on page 202.

2. You want to find out on what page the book first discusses malaria.

3. You want to find out the meaning of the word **cataclysm.**

4. You want to find out the name of the reading selection for lesson 14.

5. You want to find out the page number for the fifth selection in the book.

6. You want to find out the first page number for the topic **television.**

7. You want to find out if the word **noble** has more than one meaning in the book.

BLM 4   149

1. You've learned about three parts of a book: **the table of contents, the index,** and **the glossary.**
2. Let's review.
- What does the table of contents list? (Idea: *The selections in the book.*)
- What does the index list? (Idea: *The topics that are found in a book.*)
- What does the glossary tell? (Idea: *The meanings of words used in the book.*)
- Which book part is not in alphabetical order? (Idea: *The table of contents.*)
- Where do you find the glossary in a book? (Idea: *At the end of the book.*)
- Where do you find the table of contents? (Idea: *At the beginning of the book.*)
- Where do you find the index in a book? (Idea: *At the end of the book.*)
- If you want to find the meaning of a word that appears in the book, do you use the table of contents, the index, or the glossary? (Idea: *The glossary.*)
- If you want to find which selection begins on page 88, which part do you use? (Idea: *The table of contents.*)
- If you want to find all the places in the book that tell about the Mississippi River, which part do you use? (Idea: *The index.*)
- If you want to find name of the selection for lesson 27, which part do you use? (Idea: *The table of contents.*)
3. Look at your worksheet for lesson 4. ✔
4. For each item, you're going to write the name of the part of the book that you would use. The answer to each item is **table of contents, index,** or **glossary.** (Observe students and give feedback.)
5. (After the students complete the items, do a workcheck. Read each item, then call on a student to answer it. If the answer is wrong, give the correct answer.)

Answer Key: 1. table of contents **2.** index **3.** glossary **4.** table of contents **5.** table of contents **6.** index **7.** glossary

REFERENCE SOURCES: USING A DICTIONARY

5

Lesson 5

Name _____

Use your dictionary to find the meaning of each word. Circle the correct meaning.

1. **suppress** — The governor tried to <u>suppress</u> information about her fund raising.
   - find out
   - hold back
   - organize

2. **tedious** — The speaker gave a <u>tedious</u> explanation of how to forecast weather.
   - interesting
   - detailed
   - boring

3. **concise** — Your report should be <u>concise</u>.
   - brief
   - accurate
   - good

4. **adversary** — Why do you treat me like an <u>adversary</u>?
   - child
   - enemy
   - servant

5. **dwindle** — We saw our food supply <u>dwindle</u> each day.
   - decrease
   - rot
   - increase

6. **merge** — The two companies agreed to <u>merge</u>.
   - close
   - meet
   - combine

Copyright © SRA/McGraw-Hill. Permission is granted to reproduce this page for classroom use.

150 *BLM 5*

---

1. (Hold up a dictionary.) A **dictionary** gives the definitions, or meanings, of words. You can also use a dictionary to find out how to spell and how to pronounce words.
- The words in a dictionary are arranged in alphabetical order.
- Each page has guide words at the top. The guide word on the left side tells you the first word defined on the page. The guide word on the right side tells you the last word defined on the page.

2. Open your dictionary to page 90. ✔
- What are the guide words for page 90? (Call on a student. Accept appropriate answers.)

3. Open your dictionary to page 134. ✔
- What are the guide words for page 134? (Call on a student. Accept appropriate answers.)

4. Look at your worksheet for lesson 5. ✔

5. Word 1 is **suppress.** Here's a sentence that uses the word **suppress: The governor tried to <u>suppress</u> information about her fund raising.** From this sentence, you don't know exactly what the word means. It could mean "find out," it could mean "hold back," or it could mean "organize."
- Look up the word **suppress** and read the definition. Circle what **suppress** means. (Observe students and give feedback.)
- What does **suppress** mean? (Idea: *Hold back.*)
- I'll read what the dictionary says that **suppress** means. (Read the definition.)

6. It's your turn. Use your dictionary to find the definitions for the rest of the words. Circle the correct definition.

7. (After the students complete the items, do a workcheck. Read each word, then call on a student to give its definition. If the answer is wrong, give the correct answer.)

Answer Key: 1. hold back **2.** boring
3. brief **4.** enemy **5.** decrease **6.** combine

Lesson 6

Materials: Each student will need a copy of the worksheet for lesson 6 (Blackline Master 6); the teacher and each student will need a copy of the same children's dictionary.

REFERENCE SOURCES: USING A DICTIONARY

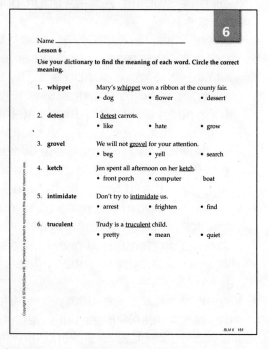

Name _____
Lesson 6
Use your dictionary to find the meaning of each word. Circle the correct meaning.

1. **whippet**   Mary's <u>whippet</u> won a ribbon at the county fair.
   • dog   • flower   • dessert

2. **detest**   I <u>detest</u> carrots.
   • like   • hate   • grow

3. **grovel**   We will not <u>grovel</u> for your attention.
   • beg   • yell   • search

4. **ketch**   Jen spent all afternoon on her <u>ketch</u>.
   • front porch   • computer   boat

5. **intimidate**   Don't try to <u>intimidate</u> us.
   • arrest   • frighten   • find

6. **truculent**   Trudy is a <u>truculent</u> child.
   • pretty   • mean   • quiet

BLM 6   151

1. (Hold up a dictionary.) Remember, a dictionary gives the definitions, or meanings, of words. It also tells you how to spell and pronounce words. The words in a dictionary are in alphabetical order. Each page has guide words at the top.
   • Open your dictionary to page 45. ✔
   • What are the guide words for page 45? (Call on a student. Accept appropriate answers.)

2. Look at your worksheet for lesson 6. ✔
3. Word 1 is **whippet.** Here's a sentence that uses the word **whippet: Mary's <u>whippet</u> won a ribbon at the county fair.** From this sentence, you don't know exactly what the word means. A whippet could be a dog, a flower, or a dessert.
4. Look up the word **whippet** in the dictionary and read the definition. Then circle what it means.
   (Observe students and give feedback.)
   • What is a **whippet**? (Idea: *A dog.*)
   • I'll read what the dictionary says that a **whippet** is. (Read the definition.)
5. It's your turn. Use your dictionary to find the definitions for the rest of the words. Circle the correct definition.
6. (After the students complete the items, do a workcheck. Read each word, then call on a student to give the definition. If the answer is wrong, give the correct answer.)

Answer Key: 1. dog **2.** hate **3.** beg **4.** boat **5.** frighten **6.** mean

Materials: Each student will need a copy of the worksheet for lesson 7 (Blackline Master 7); the teacher and each student will need a copy of the same children's dictionary.

REFERENCE SOURCES: USING A DICTIONARY

> **7**
>
> Name _____
>
> **Lesson 7**
>
> **Use your dictionary to find the correct meaning of the underlined word in each sentence. Circle the correct meaning.**
>
> 1. The new library building is <u>immense</u>.
>   • huge   • empty   • ugly
>
> 2. The company decided to <u>launch</u> its new car models at the national auto show.
>   • sell   • introduce   • drive
>
> 3. Don't be so <u>insolent.</u>
>   • slow   • stubborn   • rude
>
> 4. After they entered the theme park, Fred wanted to <u>elude</u> his big brothers.
>   • get money from   • get away from   • get food for
>
> 5. The writer of the book is <u>anonymous</u>.
>   • famous   • rich   • unknown
>
> 6. The students decided to <u>defy</u> the school dress code.
>   • disobey   • rewrite   • keep
>
> 7. Your plan to paint the room purple is <u>absurd</u>!
>   • silly   • thoughtful   • interesting
>
> 152 *BLM 7*

Copyright © SRA/McGraw-Hill. Permission is granted to reproduce this page for classroom use.

1. Look at your worksheet for lesson 7. ✔
2. For each item, you'll look up the underlined word in the dictionary. After you've found the word, read the definition. Then read the choices for definitions on your worksheet and circle the definition that's correct.

3. Item 1: **The new library building is immense.**
   • The choices for a definition are "huge," "empty," and "ugly."
   • Look up the word **immense** in your dictionary. Raise your hand when you've found it.
   • Now read the definition choices for the item to yourself. Decide which one is correct and circle it.
     (Observe students and give feedback.)
   • If the new library building is **immense,** is it huge, empty, or ugly? (Idea: *Huge.*)
4. It's your turn. Use your dictionary to find the definitions for the rest of the words. Circle the correct definition.
5. (After the students complete the items, do a workcheck. Read each word, then call on a student to give the definition. If the answer is wrong, give the correct answer.)

Answer Key: 1. huge **2.** introduce **3.** rude **4.** get away from **5.** unknown **6.** disobey **7.** silly

Lesson 8

Materials: Each student will need a copy of the worksheet for lesson 8 (Blackline Master 8) and access to an encyclopedia with an index.

REFERENCE SOURCES: USING AN ENCYCLOPEDIA

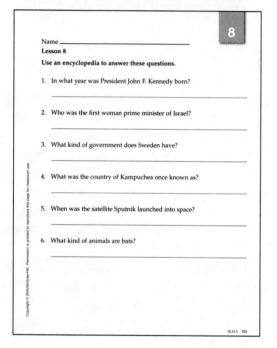

1. You've learned how to use dictionaries to find out information about words. Now let's talk about **encyclopedias,** another information resource.
- An **encyclopedia** contains information about all kinds of topics.
- An encyclopedia can be in print form as a **set of books.**
- An encyclopedia can also be in electronic form on a **CD** or as an **Internet resource.**
- Both print and electronic forms of encyclopedias arrange topics in **alphabetical order.**
- When an encyclopedia is a set of books, it has an **index** that shows the book number and the page number for each topic listed in the encyclopedia. The index is usually the last book in the set.

2. If you have access to a computer, you may want to use an electronic encyclopedia. Ask your teachers, librarians, or your parents to suggest good Internet resources.
3. Look at your worksheet for lesson 8. ✔
4. You're going to use a print encyclopedia to find the answers to some questions.
- Look at item 1: **In what year was President John F. Kennedy born**? Everybody, what topic will you look up in the index of the encyclopedia? (Signal.) *John F. Kennedy.*
- Item 2: **Who was the first woman prime minister of Israel**? Everybody, what topic will you look up? (Signal.) *Israel.*
- Item 3: **What kind of government does Sweden have**? Everybody, what topic will you look up? (Signal.) *Sweden.*
- Item 4: **What was the country of Kampuchea once known as**? Everybody, what topic will you look up? (Signal.) *Kampuchea.*
- Item 5: **When was the satellite Sputnik launched into space**? What topic will you look up? (Ideas: *Sputnik; space exploration; satellites.*)
- Item 6: **What kind of animals are bats**? (Ideas: *Bats; animals.*)
5. It's your turn. Use the encyclopedia to answer these questions.
6. (After students complete the items, do a workcheck. Read each item, then call on a student to answer it. If the answer is wrong, give the correct answer.)

Answer Key: 1. 1917 **2.** Golda Meir **3.** constitutional monarchy **4.** Cambodia **5.** October 4, 1957 **6.** mammals

Materials: Each student will need a copy of the worksheet for lesson 9 (Blackline Master 9) and access to an encyclopedia with an index.

REFERENCE SOURCES: USING AN ENCYCLOPEDIA

9

Lesson 9

Name _____

Use an encyclopedia to answer these questions.

1. In what country is the volcano Krakatoa located?
   _____

2. What is the average life span of a killer whale?
   _____

3. Who was Euripides?
   _____

4. What are some good sources of vitamin A?
   _____

5. What is the state bird of Hawaii?
   _____

6. In what year did Catherine the Great become empress of Russia?
   _____

154 BLM 9

1. Let's review what you know about encyclopedias.
- What's an encyclopedia? (Idea: *A resource that contains information about all kinds of topics.*)
- How are the topics in an encyclopedia arranged? (Idea: *In alphabetical order.*)
- What do you find in the index of an encyclopedia? (Idea: *The book number and the page number for each topic listed in the encyclopedia.*)
- Where do you find the index in a print encyclopedia? (Idea: *In the last book in the set.*)

2. Look at your worksheet for lesson 9. ✔
3. You're going to use a print encyclopedia to find the answers to the questions.
- Item 1: **In what country is the volcano Krakatoa located**? What topic will you look up in the index of the encyclopedia? (Ideas: *Krakatoa; volcanoes.*)
- Item 2: **What is the average life span of a killer whale**? What topic will you look up? (Ideas: *Killer whales; whales; oceans.*)
- Item 3: **Who was Euripides**? Everybody, what topic will you look up? (Signal.) *Euripides.*
- Item 4: **What are some good sources of vitamin A**? What topic will you look up? (Ideas: *Vitamins; nutrition; health.*)
- Item 5: **What is the state bird of Hawaii**? What topic will you look up? (Idea: *Hawaii.*)
- Item 6: **In what year did Catherine the Great become empress of Russia**? (Ideas: *Catherine the Great; Russia.*)

4. It's your turn. Use the encyclopedia to answer these questions.
5. (After students complete the items, do a workcheck. Read each item, then call on a student to answer it. If the answer is wrong, give the correct answer.)

Answer Key: 1. Indonesia **2.** 50–80 years **3.** Greek playwright **4.** Ideas: liver; eggs; cheese; dark green vegetables **5.** nene goose **6.** 1764

Lesson 10

Materials: Each student will need a copy of the worksheet for lesson 10 (Blackline Master 10) and access to an encyclopedia with an index.

REFERENCE SOURCES: USING AN ENCYCLOPEDIA

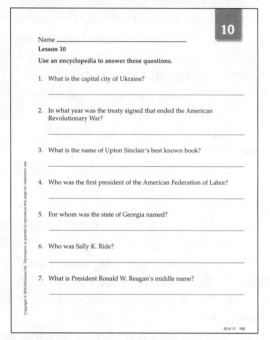

Name _____

Lesson 10

Use an encyclopedia to answer these questions.

1. What is the capital city of Ukraine?

2. In what year was the treaty signed that ended the American Revolutionary War?

3. What is the name of Upton Sinclair's best known book?

4. Who was the first president of the American Federation of Labor?

5. For whom was the state of Georgia named?

6. Who was Sally K. Ride?

7. What is President Ronald W. Reagan's middle name?

BLM 10 155

1. Look at your worksheet for lesson 10. ✔
2. Use an encyclopedia to find the answers to the questions.

- Item 1: **What is the capital city of Ukraine**? What topic will you look up in the index of the encyclopedia? (Idea: *Ukraine.*)
- Look it up in the index. Raise your hand when you've found it.
- What is the book number and page number for Ukraine? (**Call on a student. Accept accurate answers.**)
- Look it up. Raise your hand when you've found it.
- What is the capital city of Ukraine? (Idea: *Kiev.*)

3. Use the encyclopedia to answer the rest of the questions.
4. (After students complete the items, do a workcheck. Read each item, then call on a student to answer it. If the answer is wrong, give the correct answer.)

Answer Key: 1. Kiev **2.** 1783 **3.** *The Jungle* **4.** Samuel Gompers **5.** King George II of England **6.** the first American woman astronaut **7.** Wilson

Materials: Each student will need a copy of the worksheet for lesson 11 (Blackline Master 11) and access to an atlas of the United States.

REFERENCE SOURCES: USING AN ATLAS

> **11**
>
> Name _____
>
> Lesson 11
>
> **Use the United States atlas to answer these questions.**
>
> 1. Which state is directly north of Kansas?
>   _____
>
> 2. What's the capital city of Louisiana?
>   _____
>
> 3. What's the name of the tallest mountain in Connecticut?
>   _____
>
> 4. What lake is near Oshkosh, Wisconsin?
>   _____
>
> 5. Which one of the following cities is in the western part of Arkansas: Little Rock, Pine Bluff, or Fort Smith?
>   _____
>
> 6. What large body of water is near Seattle, Washington?
>   _____
>
> 156 BLM 11

1. You've learned about dictionaries and encyclopedias. Now you're going to learn about another information resource, the **atlas.**
- An **atlas** shows maps of different places and gives information about these places. In an atlas of the United States, you can use the maps to find information such as:
  - how far Oregon is from Oklahoma
  - which states border Rhode Island
  - the names of rivers in Tennessee
  - the capital city of Florida
  - the highest point in Utah
  - the largest lake in Minnesota
- An atlas has a **table of contents** at the beginning and an **index** at the end to help you find the map you're looking for.

2. Look at your worksheet for lesson 11. ✔
3. You're going to use an atlas to find the answers to some questions.
- Item 1: **Which state is directly north of Kansas?** Everybody, what will you look up in the table of contents or index? (Ideas: *Kansas*; *United States.*)
- Item 2: **What's the capital city of Louisiana?** What will you look up? (Idea: *Louisiana.*)
- Item 3: **What's the name of the tallest mountain in Connecticut?** What will you look up? (Idea: *Connecticut.*)
- Item 4: **What lake is near Oshkosh, Wisconsin?** What will you look up? (Idea: *Wisconsin.*)
- Item 5: **Which one of the following cities is in the western part of Arkansas: Little Rock, Pine Bluff, or Fort Smith?** What will you look up? (Idea: *Arkansas.*)
- Item 6: **What large body of water is near Seattle, Washington?** What will you look up? (Idea: *Washington.*)
4. It's your turn. Use the United States atlas to find the answers to these questions.
5. (After students complete the items, do a workcheck. Read each item, then call on a student to answer it. If the answer is wrong, give the correct answer.)

Answer Key: 1. Nebraska **2.** Baton Rouge **3.** Mt. Frissell **4.** Lake Winnebago **5.** Fort Smith **6.** Puget Sound

Lesson 12

REFERENCE SOURCES: USING AN ATLAS

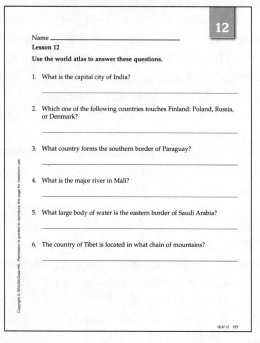

1. Let's review what you know about atlases.
- An **atlas** shows maps of different places.
- You can use the maps in an atlas to find information such as the distance from one place to another; names and locations of lakes, rivers, and mountains; capital cities.
- An atlas has a table of contents at the beginning and an index at the end to help you find the map you're looking for.
2. In the last lesson, you used an atlas of the United States to find information about places in this country. Now you're going to use a world atlas to find information about places all over the world.

3. Look at your worksheet for lesson 12. ✔
- Item 1: **What is the capital city of India?** Everybody, what will you look up in the table of contents or index? (Idea: *India.*)
- Item 2: **Which one of the following countries touches Finland: Poland, Russia, or Denmark?** What will you look up? (Ideas: *Finland; Poland; Russia; Denmark.*)
- Item 3: **What country forms the southern border of Paraguay?** What will you look up? (Idea: *Paraguay.*)
- Item 4: **What is the major river in Mali?** What will you look up? (Idea: *Mali.*)
- Item 5: **What large body of water is the eastern border of Saudi Arabia?** What will you look up? (Idea: *Saudi Arabia.*)
- Item 6: **The country of Tibet is located in what chain of mountains?** What will you look up? (Idea: *Tibet.*)
4. It's your turn. Use the world atlas to find the answers to these questions.
5. (After students complete the items, do a workcheck. Read each item, then call on a student to answer it. If the answer is wrong, give the correct answer.)

Answer Key: 1. New Delhi **2.** Russia **3.** Argentina **4.** the Niger **5.** the Persian Gulf **6.** the Himalayas

USING INFORMATION RESOURCES

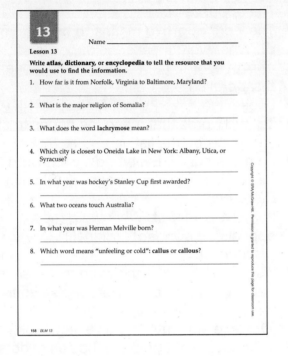

1. You've used dictionaries, encyclopedias, and atlases. Let's see what you know about when to use each information resource.
2. Find your worksheet for lesson 13. ✔
3. You'll answer each question by writing **atlas, dictionary,** or **encyclopedia** to tell the resource that you would use to find the information.
4. (After students complete the items, do a workcheck. Read each item, then call on a student to answer it. If the answer is wrong, give the correct answer.)

Answer Key: 1. atlas **2.** encyclopedia
3. dictionary **4.** atlas **5.** encyclopedia
6. atlas **7.** encyclopedia **8.** dictionary

Lesson 14

PREFIXES:
DIS

14

Name _____

Lesson 14

Write the word that means the opposite for each word on the list.

1. agree _____

2. connect _____

3. appear _____

4. like _____

5. satisfied _____

6. honor _____

7. order _____

8. prove _____

9. allow _____

Copyright © SRA/McGraw-Hill. Permission is granted to reproduce this page for classroom use.

BLM 14   159

1. A **prefix** is a word part that comes at the beginning of some words. Adding a prefix to a word changes the meaning of the word.
2. Some prefixes have a clear meaning.
- (Write on the board:)

> **dis**

- The prefix **dis** usually means **the opposite of.** When you add the prefix **dis** to word, the new word means the opposite of the old one.

- What does the prefix **dis** mean? (Signal.) *The opposite of.*
- The word **approve** means **to be in favor of.** What word means the opposite of **approve,** or to not be in favor of? (Idea: *Disapprove.*)
3. Look at your worksheet for lesson 14. ✔
- Tell the words that mean the opposite of the words on the list.
- Item 1 is **agree.** Everybody, what word means the opposite of **agree**? (Signal.) *Disagree.*
- Item 2 is **connect.** What word means the opposite of **connect**? (Signal.) *Disconnect.*
4. It's your turn. Write the word that means the opposite for each word. Raise your hand when you're finished. (Observe students and give feedback.)
5. (After students complete the items, do a workcheck. Read each word, then call on a student to give the opposite. If the answer is wrong, give the correct answer.)

Answer Key: 1. disagree **2.** disconnect
3. disappear **4.** dislike **5.** dissatisfied
6. dishonor **7.** disorder **8.** disprove
9. disallow

EXERCISE 1

PREFIXES:

RE

15

Lesson 15

Name _____

A. Write the word with the prefix that means **again.**

1. tie _____

2. sell _____

3. play _____

4. charge _____

5. group _____

B. Write words with the prefixes **dis** and **re**

	dis	re
1. locate	_____	_____
2. appear	_____	_____
3. connect	_____	_____
4. assemble	_____	_____
5. arm	_____	_____
6. mount	_____	_____

160   BLM 15

---

1. A **prefix** is a word part that comes at the beginning of words. Adding a prefix to a word changes the meaning of the word.
   - What is a prefix? (Idea: *A word part that come at the beginning of some words and changes their meaning.*)
2. You've learned a prefix that means **the opposite of.** Everybody, what's that prefix? (Signal.) *Dis.*
   - What word means the opposite of **believe**? (Idea: *Disbelieve.*)
   - What word means the opposite of **qualify**? (Idea: *Disqualify.*)
3. You're going to learn a prefix that usually means **again.**
   - (Write on the board:)

---

re

- What does **re** mean? (Idea: *Again.*)
- So **reclaim** means **to claim again.**
- What does the word **retell** mean? (Idea: *To tell again.*)
4. Look at part A on your worksheet. ✔
5. For each item, write the word with the prefix that means **again.** Raise your hand when you're finished.
   (Observe students and give feedback.)
6. (Write on the board:)

1. **retie**	4. **recharge**
2. **resell**	5. **regroup**
3. **replay**	

7. Check your work. Here's what you should have. Correct any mistakes.

EXERCISE 2

PREFIXES:

DIS AND RE

1. Look at part B on your worksheet. ✔
- For each word on the list, you're going to write words with the prefixes **dis** and **re.** Raise your hand when you're finished.
  (Observe students and give feedback.)
2. (After students complete the items, do a workcheck. Read each word, then call on a student to give the word that means **the opposite of,** then the word that means **again.** If an answer is wrong, give the correct answer.)

Answer Key: 1. dislocate; relocate
2. disappear; reappear **3.** disconnect; reconnect **4.** disassemble; reassemble
5. disarm; rearm **6.** dismount; remount

Lesson 16

EXERCISE 1
PREFIXES:
UN

Name _____

Lesson 16

A. Write the word with the prefix that means **not**.

1. comfortable _____
2. ready _____
3. reliable _____
4. met _____
5. talented _____

B. Write the word that answers the question. The word you write will have one of these prefixes: **dis**, **re**, or **un**.

1. What word means **the opposite of qualified**? _____
2. What word means **not natural**? _____
3. What word means **to direct again**? _____
4. What word means **to invent again**? _____
5. What word means **the opposite of believe**? _____
6. What word means **not scientific**? _____

BLM 16 161

1. You're going to learn a prefix that usually means **not**.
• (Write on the board:)

un

• The word **unclear** means **not clear.**
• What does the word **unhappy** mean? (Idea: *Not happy.*)
• What word means **not available**? (Idea: *Unavailable.*)
2. Look at part A on your worksheet for lesson 16. ✔
• For each item, write the word with the prefix that means **not.** Raise your hand when you're finished. **(Observe students and give feedback.)**

3. (Write on the board:)

1. **uncomfortable**
2. **unready**
3. **unreliable**
4. **unmet**
5. **untalented**

4. Here's what you should have. Correct any mistakes.

EXERCISE 2
PREFIXES

1. Let's review the prefixes you've learned.
• What prefix means **the opposite of**? (Idea: *Dis.*)
• What prefix means **again**? **(Idea: *Re.*)**
• What is one prefix that means **not**? (Idea: *Un.*)
2. Find part B on your worksheet. ✔
• Write the word that answers the question. The word you write will have one of the prefixes **dis, re,** or **un.** Raise your hand when you're finished. **(Observe students and give feedback.)**
3. (After students complete the items, do a workcheck.)
4. (Read each item, then call on a student to give the answer. If an answer is wrong, give the correct answer.)

Answer Key: 1. disqualified **2.** unnatural **3.** redirect **4.** reinvent **5.** disbelieve **6.** unscientific

Materials: Each student will need a copy of the worksheet for lesson 17 (Blackline Master 17); the teacher and each student will need a copy of the same children's dictionary.

EXERCISE 1

PREFIXES:

PRE

17
Lesson 17
Name _____

A. Write the word with the prefix that means **before.**

1. writing _____
2. determine _____
3. school _____
4. trial _____
5. order _____

B. Circle the correct word. Use your dictionary to check your answers.

1. Jason and Jordan look alike, but they have very **dissimilar, unsimilar** personalities.
2. Our TV show is so popular, we will **prebroadcast, rebroadcast** it three more times.
3. As Paul sped down the long hill, his bike chain came **disattached, unattached.**
4. It's a good idea to **preplan, replan** for college while you're in high school.

182 BLM 17

1. You're going to learn another prefix. This prefix usually means **before.**
• (Write on the board:)

> **pre**

• The word **predawn** means **before dawn.** The word **presort** means **to sort before.**
• What does the word **presale** mean? (Idea: *Before the sale.*)
• What does the word **premix** mean? (Idea: *To mix before.*)
• What word means **to arrange before**? (Idea: *Prearrange.*)
2. Look at part A on your worksheet for lesson 17. ✔

• For each item on the list, write the word with the prefix that means **before.** Raise your hand when you're finished. (Observe students and give feedback.)
3. (After students complete the items, do a workcheck.)
4. (Read each item, then call on a student to give the answer. If an answer is wrong, give the correct answer.)

Answer Key: 1. prewriting **2.** predetermine **3.** preschool **4.** pretrial **5.** preorder

EXERCISE 2

PREFIXES

1. What prefix means **the opposite of**? (Signal.) *Dis.*
• What prefix means **again**? (Signal.) *Re.*
• What prefix means **before**? (Signal.) *Pre.*
• What is one prefix that means **not**? (Signal.) *Un.*
2. Find part B on your worksheet. ✔
• Circle the correct word. Use your dictionary to check your answers. Raise your hand when you're finished. (Observe students and give feedback.)
3. (Write on the board:)

> **1. dissimilar   3. unattached**
> **2. rebroadcast   4. preplan**

4. Here's what you should have. Correct any mistakes.

Lesson 18

Materials: Each student will need a copy of the worksheet for lesson 18 (Blackline Master 18); the teacher and each student will need a copy of the same children's dictionary.

PREFIXES:
IN

Name _____
Lesson 18

Write the word with the prefix that means **not**. Use your dictionary to check your answers.

1. prepared _____
2. sane _____
3. justice _____
4. helpful _____
5. accurate _____
6. imaginable _____
7. gracious _____
8. human _____
9. exact _____

BLM 18   163

1. You've learned a prefix that means **not**. Everybody, what's that prefix? **(Signal.)** *Un.*
- What word means **not certain**? **(Idea:** *Uncertain.***)**
- What does the word **unimportant** mean? **(Idea:** *Not important.***)**
2. You're going to learn another prefix that also means **not**.
3. (Write on the board:)

in

- The word **incorrect** means **not correct**. The word **incomplete** means **not complete**.
- What does the word **inactive** mean? **(Idea:** *Not active.***)**

- What does the word **infrequent** mean? **(Idea:** *Not frequent.***)**
- What word means **not effective**? **(Idea:** *Ineffective.***)**
- If you're not sure whether the prefix for a word should be **un** or **in,** use a dictionary.
4. Which word means **not able: inable** or **unable**? Use the dictionary. Look up the word you think is right. If you don't find it, look up the other word. Raise your hand when you've found the right word.
- Which word means **not able**? **(Idea:** *Unable.***)**
- Which word means **not formal: informal** or **unformal**? Raise your hand when you've found the right word.
- Which word means **not formal**? **(Idea:** *Informal.***)**
5. Look at your worksheet for lesson 18. ✔
- For each item, write the word with the prefix that means **not**. Use your dictionary to check your answers. (Observe students and give feedback.)
6. (Write on the board:)

1. **unprepared**	6. **unimaginable**
2. **insane**	7. **ungracious**
3. **injustice**	8. **inhuman**
4. **unhelpful**	9. **inexact**
5. **inaccurate**	

7. Here's what you should have. Correct any mistakes.

Materials: Each student will need a copy of the worksheet for lesson 19 (Blackline Master 19); the teacher and each student will need a copy of the same children's dictionary.

EXERCISE 1

PREFIXES:

MULTI

19

Lesson 19

Name _____

A. Write a word with the prefix that means **many** to complete each sentence.

1. national   The president attended a _____ conference.

2. media   The _____ concert was broadcast over TV, radio, and the Internet.

3. lane   The state plans to build a _____ highway near our home.

4. cultural   Our school has a wide choice of _____ courses.

5. stage   The trip to Mars required the use of a _____ rocket.

B. Write the word that answers the question. The word you write will have one of these prefixes: **dis, re, un, pre, in,** or **multi.** Use your dictionary to check your answers.

1. What word means **not known?**   _____

2. What word means **the opposite of honor?**   _____

3. What word means **to decorate again?**   _____

4. What word means **not convenient?**   _____

5. What word means **many units?**   _____

6. What word means **to pay before?**   _____

164 BLM 19

1. You're going to learn another prefix. This prefix means **many.**
2. (Write on the board:)

> **multi**

- Someone who is **multitalented** has many talents.
- What is the word for something with many colors? (Idea: *Multicolored.*)
- What is a **multipurpose** room? (Idea: *A room with many purposes.*)

3. Look at part A on your worksheet for lesson 19. ✔

- Write a word that means **many** to complete each sentence. (Observe students and give feedback.)

4. (After students complete the items, do a workcheck.)

5. (For each item, call on a student to give the answer. If an answer is wrong, give the correct answer.)

Answer Key: 1. multinational **2.** multimedia **3.** multilane **4.** multicultural **5.** multistage

EXERCISE 2

PREFIXES

1. Find part B on your worksheet. ✔
- Write the word that answers the question. The word you write will have one of the prefixes **dis, re, un, pre,** or **multi.** Use your dictionary to check your answers. Raise your hand when you're finished. (Observe students and give feedback.)
2. (Write on the board:)

> 1. **unknown**   4. **inconvenient**
> 2. **dishonor**   5. **multiunit**
> 3. **redecorate**   6. **prepay**

3. Here's what you should have. Correct any mistakes.

Lesson 20

EXERCISE 1

PREFIXES: SUPER

Name _____
Lesson 20

A. Write a word that means **very** or **more than** to complete each sentence

1. **strong**   The weightlifter was _____.
2. **power**   The United States is a _____.
3. **human**   To win the race took a _____ effort.
4. **rich**   Only the _____ can afford to live here.
5. **charged**   Greg's car has a _____ engine.

B. Circle the correct word. Use your dictionary to check your answers.

1. The hotel towels are **multisoft, supersoft.**
2. The noise was so loud, it was absolutely **unbearable, disbearable.**
3. We **prearranged, unarranged** our trip to Mexico almost a year ago.
4. After falling at the starting block, the runner got up and **preentered, reentered** the race.
5. You can't **disprove, unprove** what I told you.
6. The town doesn't need another **multistory, superstory** building.
7. The cab driver took the most **indirect, undirect** way to the airport.

BLM 20 165

1. (Write on the board:)

> **super**

2. This prefix means **more than** or **very.**
- A **superhero** is someone who is more than a hero.
- Sugar that is very fine is **superfine.**
- What is a **supersensitive** person? (Idea: *Someone who is very sensitive.*)
- What word means **more than clean**? (Idea: *Superclean.*)
3. Look at part A on your worksheet for lesson 20. ✔
- For each item, write the word that means **very** or **more than.**
(Observe students and give feedback.)

4. (Write on the board:)

> 1. **superstrong**   4. **superrich**
> 2. **superpower**   5. **supercharged**
> 3. **superhuman**

5. Here's what you should have. Correct any mistakes.

EXERCISE 2

PREFIXES

1. Let's review the prefixes you've learned.
- What prefix means **very** or **more than**? (Signal.) *Super.*
- What prefix means **the opposite of**? (Signal.) *Dis.*
- What prefix means **before**? (Signal.) *Pre.*
- What prefix means **again**? (Signal.) *Re.*
- What is one prefix that means **not**? (Ideas: *Un or in.*)
- What is another prefix that means **not**? (Ideas: *In or un.*)
- What prefix means **many**? (Idea: *Multi.*)
2. Find part B on your worksheet. ✔
- Circle the correct word. Use your dictionary to check your answers. Raise your hand when you're finished.
(Observe students and give feedback.)
3. (After students complete the items, do a workcheck.)
4. (For each item, call on a student to give the answer. If an answer is wrong, give the correct answer.)

Answer Key: 1. supersoft **2.** unbearable
3. prearranged **4.** reentered **5.** disprove
6. multistory **7.** indirect

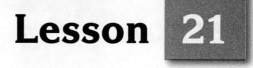

Materials: Each student will need a copy of the worksheet for lesson 21 (Blackline Master 21); the teacher and each student will need a copy of the same children's dictionary.

SUFFIXES: LESS

21

Name _____

Lesson 21

Write the word with the suffix that means **without.**

1. weight _____
2. effort _____
3. age _____
4. shape _____
5. home _____
6. clue _____
7. color _____
8. sound _____
9. worth _____

166 BLM 21

---

1. You know that some parts appear at the beginnings of words and change the meaning of a word. Everybody, what are these parts called? (Signal.) *Prefixes.*
2. There are also parts that appear at the ends of words. These parts are called **suffixes.**
   - What are parts at the ends of words called? (Signal.) *Suffixes.*
   - Suffixes can also change the meaning of a word.
3. (Write on the board:)

   less

   - The suffix **less** usually means **without.**
   - What does the suffix **less** mean? (Signal.) *Without.*

   - The word **hopeless** means **without hope.** The word **thoughtless** means **without thought.**
   - What does the word **careless** mean? (Idea: *Without care.*)
   - If you're without fear, what are you? (Idea: *Fearless.*)
   - What word means **without joy**? (Idea: *Joyless.*)
4. Look at your worksheet for lesson 21. ✔
5. For each item, write the word with the suffix that means **without.** Raise your hand when you're finished. (Observe students and give feedback.)
6. (After students complete the items, do a workcheck.)
7. (Read each item, then call on a student to give the answer. If an answer is wrong, give the correct answer.)

Answer Key: 1. weightless **2.** effortless **3.** ageless **4.** shapeless **5.** homeless **6.** clueless **7.** colorless **8.** soundless **9.** worthless

Lesson 22

SUFFIXES: FUL

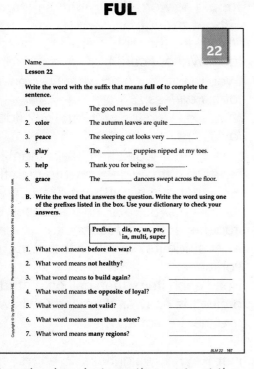

1. Everybody, what are the parts at the end of words called? (Signal.) *Suffixes.*
- What does the suffix **less** mean? (Idea: *Without.*)
2. Here's another suffix. (Write on the board:)

ful

- The suffix **ful** usually means **full of.**
- What does the suffix **ful** mean? (Signal.) *Full of.*
- The word **hopeful** means **full of hope.** The word **thoughtful** means **full of thought.**
- What word means **full of care**? (Idea: *Careful.*)
- If you're **joyful,** what are you? (Idea: *Full of joy.*)

- What does the word **fearful** mean? (Idea: *Full of fear.*)
3. Look at part A on your worksheet for lesson 22. ✔
- Write a word that means **full of** to complete each sentence. Raise your hand when you're finished. **(Observe students and give feedback.)**
4. (After students complete the items, do a workcheck.)
5. (Read each item, then call on a student to give the answer. If an answer is wrong, give the correct answer.)

Answer Key: Part A: 1. cheerful **2.** colorful **3.** peaceful **4.** playful **5.** helpful **6.** graceful

EXERCISE 2

PREFIXES

1. Find part B on your worksheet. ✔
- Write the word that answers the question. Write the word using one of the prefixes listed in the box. Use your dictionary to check your answers. Raise your hand when you're finished. **(Observe students and give feedback.)**
2. (Write on the board:)

1. **prewar**	5. **invalid**
2. **unhealthy**	6. **superstore**
3. **rebuild**	7. **multiregion**
4. **disloyal**	

3. Here's what you should have. Correct any mistakes.

Materials: Each student will need a copy of the worksheet for lesson 23 (Blackline Master 23).

EXERCISE 1
SUFFIXES:
NESS

> ### 23
> Lesson 23
> Name _____
>
> **A.** Write the word with the suffix that means **being**.
> 1. cold _____
> 2. smooth _____
> 3. mean _____
> 4. weak _____
> 5. good _____
>
> **B.** Write the word that answers the question. Write the word using one of the suffixes you've learned. Use your dictionary to check your answers.
> 1. What word means **without a name**? _____
> 2. What word means **full of shame**? _____
> 3. What word means **without motion**? _____
> 4. What word means **being bold**? _____
> 5. What word means **full of doubt**? _____
> 6. What word means **full of meaning**? _____
> 7. What word means **being smug**? _____
>
> 168 BLM 23

1. Here's another suffix. (Write on the board:)

ness

- The suffix **ness** usually means **being**.
- The word **sadness** means **being sad**. The word **brightness** means **being bright**.
- What word means **being soft**? (Idea: *Softness.*)
- What does the word **rudeness** mean? (Idea: *Being rude.*)

2. Look at part A on your worksheet for lesson 23. ✔

- For each item, write the word with the suffix that means **being.** Raise your hand when you're finished.
  (Observe students and give feedback.)
3. (After students complete the items, do a workcheck.)
4. (Read each item, then call on a student to give the answer. If an answer is wrong, give the correct answer.)

Answer Key: 1. coldness **2.** smoothness **3.** meanness **4.** weakness **5.** goodness

EXERCISE 2
SUFFIXES
1. Let's review the suffixes you've learned.
- What suffix means **without**? (Signal.) *Less.*
- What suffix means **full of**? (Signal.) *Ful.*
- What suffix means **being**? (Signal.) *Ness.*
2. Find part B on your worksheet. ✔
- Write the word that answers the question. Write the word using one of the suffixes you've learned. Raise your hand when you're finished.
  (Observe students and give feedback.)
3. (Write on the board:)

1. **nameless**	5. **doubtful**
2. **shameful**	6. **meaningful**
3. **motionless**	7. **smugness**
4. **boldness**	

4. Here's what you should have. Correct any mistakes.

Lesson 24

EXERCISE 1

SUFFIXES:

ER

Name _____

24

Lesson 24

A. Write the word with the suffix that means **one who** to complete the sentence.

1. **read**   Benny is an avid _____.

2. **pitch**   Who wants to be the _____ for the first ball game?

3. **send**   I wrote "return to _____" on the letter and dropped it in the mailbox.

4. **lead**   James is the _____ of our new club.

5. **design**   Samantha's dress was made especially for her by a world-famous clothing _____.

B. Write the word that answers the question. Write the word using one of the prefixes or suffixes you've learned. Use your dictionary to check your answers.

1. What word means **not kind**?   _____

2. What word means **to view before**?   _____

3. What word means **full of respect**?   _____

4. What word means **not decisive**?   _____

5. What word means **one who prints**?   _____

6. What word means **without harm**?   _____

7. What word means **being tough**?   _____

8. What word means **the opposite of allow**?   _____

BLM 24   169

1. (Write on the board:)

er

- The suffix **er** sometimes means **one who.**
- The word for **one who talks** is **talker.** The word for **one who builds** is **builder.**
- What's the word for **one who thinks**? (Idea: *Thinker.*)
- What's a teacher? (Idea: *One who teaches.*)
- What's word means **one who paints**? (Idea: *Painter.*)

2. Look at part A on your worksheet for lesson 24. ✔

- For each item, write the word with the suffix that means **one who** to complete the sentence. Raise your hand when you're finished. (Observe students and give feedback.)

3. (After students complete the items, do a workcheck.)

4. (For each item, call on a student to say the word and read the sentence. If an answer is wrong, give the correct answer.)

Answer Key: 1. reader **2.** pitcher **3.** sender **4.** leader **5.** designer

EXERCISE 2

PREFIXES AND SUFFIXES

1. Find part B on your worksheet. ✔

- Write the word that answers the question. Write the word using one of the prefixes or suffixes you've learned. Use your dictionary to check your answers. Raise your hand when you're finished. (Observe students and give feedback.)

2. (Write on the board:)

1. **unkind**	5. **printer**
2. **preview**	6. **harmless**
3. **respectful**	7. **toughness**
4. **indecisive**	8. **disallow**

3. Here's what you should have. Correct any mistakes.

Materials: Each student will need a copy of the worksheet for lesson 25 (Blackline Master 25); the teacher and each student will need a copy of the same children's dictionary.

EXERCISE 1

SUFFIXES: ABLE, IBLE

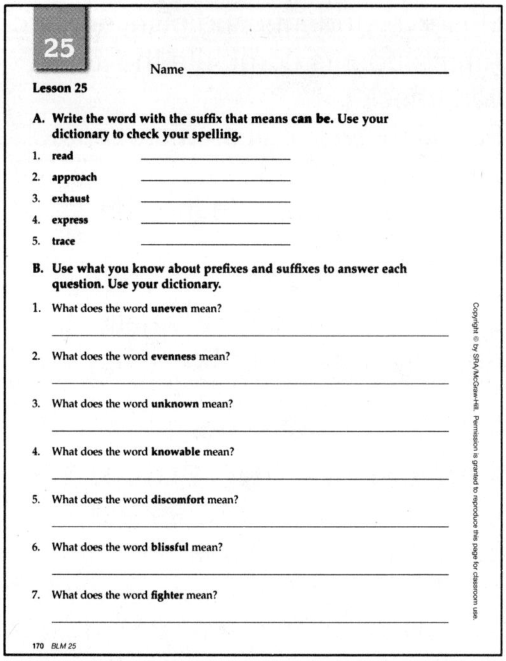
25

Lesson 25

Name ____________

A. Write the word with the suffix that means can be. Use your dictionary to check your spelling.

1. **read** ____________
2. **approach** ____________
3. **exhaust** ____________
4. **express** ____________
5. **trace** ____________

B. Use what you know about prefixes and suffixes to answer each question. Use your dictionary.

1. What does the word **uneven** mean?
2. What does the word **evenness** mean?
3. What does the word **unknown** mean?
4. What does the word **knowable** mean?
5. What does the word **discomfort** mean?
6. What does the word **blissful** mean?
7. What does the word **fighter** mean?

Copyright © by SRA/McGraw-Hill. Permission is granted to reproduce this page for classroom use.

170 *BLM 25*

1. (Write on the board:)

able, ible

- The suffix **able** usually means **can be.** This suffix can also be spelled **ible,** so you'll have to use a dictionary to check which spelling to use.
- The word **breakable** means **can be broken.** The word **avoidable** means **can be avoided.** The word **resistible** means **can be resisted.**
- What word means **can be used**? (Idea: *Usable.*)
- What does the word **stretchable** mean? (Idea: *Can be stretched.*)

2. Look at part A on your worksheet for lesson 25. ✔
- For each item, write the word with the suffix that means **can be.** Use your dictionary to check the spelling of the words. Raise your hand when you're finished.
(Observe students and give feedback.)
3. (Write on the board:)

1. **readable**	4. **expressible**
2. **approachable**	5. **traceable**
3. **exhaustible**	

4. Here's what you should have. Check your spelling. Correct any mistakes.

EXERCISE 2

PREFIXES AND SUFFIXES

1. Find part B on your worksheet. ✔
- Use what you know about prefixes and suffixes to answer the questions. Use your dictionary. Raise your hand when you're finished.
(Observe students and give feedback.)
2. (After students complete the items, do a workcheck.)
3. (Read each item, then call on a student to give the answer. If an answer is wrong, give the correct answer.)

Answer Key: **1.** not even **2.** being even **3.** not known **4.** can be known **5.** without comfort **6.** full of bliss **7.** one who fights

Lesson 26

EXERCISE 1
SUFFIXES:
LY

Name _____

Lesson 26

26

A. Write the word with the suffix that means **in a certain way** to complete the sentence.

1. quick   Barb walked _____ to the park.

2. brief   Hank paused _____ before he entered the room.

3. extreme   José was _____ upset when you didn't call him.

4. active   Harriet is _____ involved in several community groups.

5. sweet   The children sang _____.

B. Write the word that answers the question. Write the word using one of the prefixes or suffixes you've learned. Use your dictionary to check your answers.

1. What word means **in a faint way**?   _____

2. What word means **one who dances**?   _____

3. What word means **full of power**?   _____

4. What word means **being small**?   _____

5. What word means **without end**?   _____

6. What word means **can be reversed**?   _____

7. What word means **to cut before**?   _____

8. What word means **the opposite of claim**? _____

9. What word means **without humor**?   _____

10. What word means **can be replaced**?   _____

BLM 26   171

1. (Write on the board:)

ly

- The suffix **ly** sometimes means **in a certain way.**
- The word for **in a pleasant way** is **pleasantly.** The word for **in a quiet way** is **quietly.**
- What's the word for **in a weak way**? (Idea: *Weakly.*)
- What does **oddly** mean? (Idea: *In an odd way.*)

2. Look at part A on your worksheet for lesson 26. ✔

- For each item, write the word with the suffix that means **in a certain way** to complete the sentence. Raise your hand when you're finished.
  (Observe students and give feedback.)

3. (After students complete the items, do a workcheck.)

4. (For each item, call on a student to say the word and read the sentence. If an answer is wrong, give the correct answer.)

Answer Key: **1.** quickly **2.** briefly **3.** extremely **4.** actively **5.** sweetly

EXERCISE 2
PREFIXES AND SUFFIXES

1. Find part B on your worksheet. ✔
- Write the word that answers the question. Write the word using one of the prefixes or suffixes you've learned. Use your dictionary to check your answers. Raise your hand when you're finished. (Observe students and give feedback.)

2. (Write on the board:)

1. faintly	6. reversible
2. dancer	7. precut
3. powerful	8. disclaim
4. smallness	9. humorless
5. endless	10. replaceable

3. Here's what you should have. Check your spelling. Correct any mistakes.

ROOT WORDS

> **27**
>
> Lesson 27
>
> Name _____
>
> Underline the prefix, circle the root, and draw a line over the suffix. Then write the meaning of the word. Use your dictionary.
>
> 1. disprove
> Meaning: _____
> 2. changeable
> Meaning: _____
> 3. untruthful
> Meaning: _____
> 4. infrequently
> Meaning: _____
> 5. nearness
> Meaning: _____
> 6. pretrial
> Meaning: _____
> 7. gatherer
> Meaning: _____
> 8. close
> Meaning: _____
>
> 172 BLM 27

1. (Write on the board:)

   > 1. **disprove**
   > 2. **changeable**
   > 3. **untruthful**

2. You know **prefixes** come at the beginnings of words. You also know **suffixes** come at the ends of words.
3. The word, or part of a word, that you add prefixes or suffixes to is called the **root.** Everybody, to what do you add prefixes and suffixes? (Signal.) *The root.*
4. Sometimes the root is a complete word.
- Look at word 1: **Disprove.**
- Does **disprove** have a prefix? (Signal.) *Yes.*
- What's the prefix? (Signal.) *Dis.*
- Does it have a suffix? (Signal.) *No.*

- What's the root? (Signal.) *Prove.*
- Is the root a complete word? (Signal.) *Yes.*
- What does the word **disprove** mean? (Idea: *The opposite of prove.*)
5. Look at word 2: **Changeable.**
- Does **changeable** have a prefix? (Signal.) *No.*
- Does it have a suffix? (Signal.) *Yes.*
- What's the suffix? (Signal.) *Able.*
- What's the root of **changeable**? (Signal.) *Change.*
- Is that a complete word? (Signal.) *Yes.*
- What does the word **changeable** mean? (Idea: *Can be changed.*)
6. Word 3 is **untruthful.**
- Does it have a prefix? (Signal.) *Yes.*
- What's the prefix? (Signal.) *Un.*
- Does it have a suffix? (Signal.) *Yes.*
- What's the suffix? (Signal.) *Ful.*
- What's the root? (Signal.) *Truth.*
- Is that a complete word? (Signal.) *Yes.*
- What does **untruthful** mean? (Idea: *Not full of truth.*)
7. Look at your worksheet for lesson 27. ✔
- The directions tell you to underline each prefix, circle the root, and draw a line over the suffix. Then write what the word means. Use your dictionary.
- Remember, not every word has a prefix, so you won't underline a word part in every word. Also, not every word has a suffix, so you won't draw a line over a word part in every word. However, all words have a root, so you'll circle something in every word.
(Observe students and give feedback.)
8. (After students complete the items, do a workcheck.)

9. (Call on a student for each item and ask: What did you underline? What did you circle? What did you draw a line over? What's the meaning of the word? If an answer is wrong, give the correct answer.)

Answer Key: 1. dis(prove); the opposite of prove **2.** (change)able; can be changed **3.** un(truth)ful; not full of truth; **4.** in(frequent)ly; not in a frequent way **5.** (near)ness; being near **6.** pre(trial); before the trial **7.** (gather)er; one who gathers **8.** (close); near

Lesson 28

Materials: Each student will need a copy of the worksheet for lesson 28 (Blackline Master 28); the teacher and each student will need a copy of the same children's dictionary.

ROOT WORDS

> **28**
>
> Name _____
> Lesson 28
>
> **Underline the prefix, circle the root, and draw a line over the suffix. Then write the meaning of the word. Use your dictionary.**
>
> 1. shyness
>
> Meaning: _____
>
> 2. guiltless
>
> Meaning: _____
>
> 3. indirectly
>
> Meaning: _____
>
> 4. unskillful
>
> Meaning: _____
>
> 5. reoccur
>
> Meaning: _____
>
> 6. briskly
>
> Meaning: _____
>
> 7. multimedia
>
> Meaning: _____
>
> Copyright © by SRA/McGraw-Hill. Permission is granted to reproduce this page for classroom use.
>
> BLM 28   173

1. (Write on the board:)

> 1. **shyness**
> 2. **guiltless**

2. Everybody, what do you call the word or word part to which you add prefixes and suffixes? (Signal.) *The root.*
3. Sometimes the root is a complete word.
- Look at word 1: **shyness.**
- Does **shyness** have a prefix? (Signal.) *No.*
- Does it have a suffix? (Signal.) *Yes.*
- What's the root of **shyness**? (Signal.) *Shy.*
- Is that a complete word? (Signal.) *Yes.*
- What does **shyness** mean? (Idea: *Being shy.*)
4. Look at word 2: **guiltless.**
- Does **guiltless** have a prefix? (Signal.) *No.*

- Does it have a suffix? (Signal.) *Yes.*
- What's the suffix? (Signal.) *Less.*
- What's the root of **guiltless**?(Signal.) *Guilt.*
- Is that a complete word? (Signal.) *Yes.*
- What does **guiltless** mean? (Idea: *Without guilt.*)
5. Look at your worksheet for lesson 28. ✔
- For each item, underline the prefix, circle the root, and draw a line over the suffix. The write the meaning of the word. Use your dictionary.
- Remember, all words have a root, so you'll circle something in every word. (Observe students and give feedback.)
6. (After students complete the items, do a workcheck.)
7. (Call on a student for each item and ask: What did you underline? What did you circle? What did you draw a line over? What's the meaning of the word? If an answer is wrong, give the correct answer.)

Answer Key: 1. s̲h̲y̲ness; being shy **2.** guiltless; without guilt **3.** in̲direct̲ly not in a direct way **4.** un̲skill̲ful; not full of skill **5.** re̲occur; to occur again **6.** brisk̲ly; in a brisk way **7.** multi̲media; many media

Lesson 29

Materials: Each student will need a copy of the worksheet for lesson 29 (Blackline Master 29); the teacher and each student will need a copy of the same children's dictionary.

ROOT WORDS

29	Name _____

Lesson 29

ROOTS			
aud	hear	dict	speak, tell
cred	believe	vis	see

Use the information in the box and what you've learned about prefixes and suffixes to write the meanings of the words.

1. **audible**

Meaning: _____

2. **inaudible**

Meaning: _____

3. **predictable**

Meaning: _____

4. **visible**

Meaning: _____

5. **invisible**

Meaning: _____

6. **credible**

Meaning: _____

7. **incredible**

Meaning: _____

174 BLM 29

1. What do you call the word, or part of a word, to which you add prefixes and suffixes? (Signal.) *The root.*
2. (Write on the board:)

   1. **revisit**
   2. **predict**

3. Sometimes the root is a complete word.
- Look at word 1: **revisit.**
- Does **revisit** have a prefix? (Signal.) *Yes.*
- What's the prefix? (Idea: *Re.*)
- Does it have a suffix? (Signal.) *No.*
- What's the root of **revisit**? (Idea: *Visit.*)
- Is that a complete word? (Signal.) *Yes.*
4. But sometimes the root is not a complete word.
- Look at word 2: **predict.**
- Does **predict** have a prefix? (Signal.) *Yes.*

- What's the prefix? (Idea: *Pre.*)
- Does it have a suffix? (Signal.) *No.*
- What's the root of **predict**? (Idea: *Dict.*)
- Is that a complete word? (Signal.) *No.*
- No, **dict** is not a complete word. It comes from a very old language called **Latin. Dict** is from the Latin word meaning **speak** or **tell.**
- What does the word **predict** mean? (Idea: *To tell before.*)
- That's right. If you predict something, you tell it before it happens.
5. Look at your worksheet for lesson 29. ✔
- The box shows some common roots and their meanings. Follow along as I read:

ROOTS			
aud	hear	**dict**	speak tell
cred	believe	**vis**	see

6. Use the information in the box and what you've learned about prefixes and suffixes to write the meanings of the words.
- Word 1 is **audible.**
- Does it have a prefix? (Signal.) *No.*
- Does it have a suffix? (Signal.) *Yes.*
- What's the suffix? (Idea: *Ible.*)
- What does the suffix mean? (Idea: *Can be.*)
- What's the root? (Idea: *Aud.*)
- What does **aud** mean? (Idea: *Hear.*)
- What does the word **audible** mean? (Idea: *Can be heard.*)
- That's right. If something is audible, it can be heard.

7. Item 2 is **inaudible.**
- What's the prefix? (Idea: *In.*)
- What does **in** mean? (Idea: *Not.*)
- What does **inaudible** mean? (Idea: *Can't be heard.*)
- That's right. If something is inaudible, it can't be heard.

8. It's your turn. Write the meanings for the rest of the words. Use your dictionary. (Observe students and give feedback.)

9. (After students complete the items, do a workcheck.)

10. (Call on a student for each item and ask: What is the root? What does the root mean? What's the meaning of the word? If an answer is wrong, give the correct answer.)

Answer Key: 1. can be heard **2.** can't be heard **3.** can be told before **4.** can be seen **5.** can't be seen **6.** can be believed **7.** can't be believed

Lesson 30

ROOT WORDS

Name _____

Lesson 30

30

ROOTS			
equi	equal	port	carry
flex	bend	volv	turn, roll

Use the information in the box and what you've learned about prefixes and suffixes to write the meanings of the words.

1. **flexible**

Meaning: _____

2. **inflexible**

Meaning: _____

3. **revolve**

Meaning: _____

4. **portable**

Meaning: _____

5. **porter**

Meaning: _____

6. **equitable**

Meaning: _____

7. **inequitable**

Meaning: _____

BLM 30   175

1. Let's review the roots you've learned.
- What does the root **aud** mean? (Idea: *Hear.*)
- What does the word **audible** mean? (Idea: *Can be heard.*)
- What does the root **cred** mean? (Idea: *Believe.*)
- What does the word **incredible** mean? (Idea: *Can't be believed.*)
- What does the root **vis** mean? (Idea: *See.*)
- What does the word **visible** mean? (Idea: *Can be seen.*)
- What does the root **dict** mean? (Idea: *Speak or tell.*)
- So what does the word **predictable** mean? (Idea: *Can be told before.*)
2. Look at your worksheet for lesson 30. ✔

- The box shows some more common roots and their meanings. Follow along as I read:

ROOTS			
equi	equal	**port**	carry
flex	bend	**volv**	turn, roll

3. Use the information in the box and what you've learned about prefixes and suffixes to write the meanings of the words.
- Word 1 is **flexible.**
- Does it have a prefix? (Signal.) *No.*
- Does it have a suffix? (Signal.) *Yes.*
- What's the suffix? (Signal.) *Ible.*
- What does the suffix mean? (Idea: *Can be.*)
- What's the root? (Signal.) *Flex*
- What does **flex** mean? (Idea: *Bend.*)
- What does the word **flexible** mean? (Idea: *Can bend.*)
- Yes. If something is flexible, it can bend.
4. Word 2 is **inflexible.**
- What's the prefix? (Signal.) *In.*
- What does **in** mean? (Idea: *Not.*)
- What does **inflexible** mean? (Idea: *Can't bend.*)
- That's right. If something is **inflexible,** it can't bend.
5. It's your turn. Write the meanings for the rest of the words. Use your dictionary. **(Observe students and give feedback.)**

6. (After students complete the items, do a workcheck.)

7. Call on a student for each item and ask: What is the root? What does the root mean? What's the meaning of the word? If an answer is wrong, give the correct answer.)

Answer Key: 1. can bend **2.** can't bend **3.** turn again **4.** can be carried **5.** one who carries **6.** can be equal **7.** can't be equal

Lesson 31

Each student will need a copy of the worksheet for lesson 31 (Blackline Master 31); the teacher and each student will need a copy of the same children's dictionary.

HOMOGRAPHS

31

Name _____

Lesson 31

Use your dictionary to find the meanings of the homographs. Write two meanings for each word.

A. light

1. _____
2. _____

B. train

3. _____
4. _____

C. tick

5. _____
6. _____

D. down

7. _____
8. _____

E. hail

9. _____
10. _____

176 BLM 31

1. Some words are spelled the same but have different meanings. The name for these words is **homographs.**
- Everybody, what's the name for words that are spelled the same but have different meanings? (Signal.) *Homographs.*
2. Here are some homographs. (Write on the board:)

   1. **fast**
   2. **jar**

- Word 1 is **fast.** One meaning of the word **fast** is **speedy.** Another meaning of the word **fast** is **to go without food.**
- Word 2 is **jar.** One meaning of the word **jar** is **to rattle or shake up.** Another meaning of the word **jar** is **container.**

3. Look at your worksheet for lesson 31. ✔
- You're going to look up each homograph in a dictionary. Then you'll write two meanings for each one.
4. Word A is **light.** Look up **light** in your dictionary. Raise your hand when you've found it.
- What's one meaning of the word **light**? (Idea: *Not heavy; not dark.*)
- Write that meaning of the word.
- What's another meaning of **light**? (Idea: *Not dark; not heavy.*)
- Write that meaning of the word **light.**
5. Use your dictionary to find the meanings for the rest of the words. Write two meanings for each word. Raise your hand when you're finished.
6. (After the students complete the items, do a workcheck. For each item, call on a student to read the two meanings. If the answer is wrong, give the correct answer.)

Answer Key (Ideas): 1. not heavy **2.** not dark **3.** a vehicle **4.** to teach **5.** the sound of a clock **6.** an insect **7.** the opposite of **up 8.** soft feathers **9.** pieces of ice falling like rain **10.** a welcoming call

HOMOGRAPHS

> 32
>
> Name _____
> Lesson 32
>
> **Use your dictionary to find the meanings of the homographs. Write two meanings for each word.**
>
> **A. sock**
>
> 1. _____
> 2. _____
>
> **B. palm**
>
> 3. _____
> 4. _____
>
> **C. well**
>
> 5. _____
> 6. _____
>
> **D. lean**
>
> 7. _____
> 8. _____
>
> **E. stern**
>
> 9. _____
> 10. _____
>
> BLM 32   177

1. Everybody, what's the name for words that are spelled the same but have different meanings? **(Signal.)** *Homographs.*

2. Here are some more homographs. **(Write on the board:)**

   1. **pen**
   2. **jet**

- Word 1 is **pen.** One meaning of the word **pen** is **enclosed place.** Another meaning of the word **pen** is **writing instrument.**
- Word 2 is **jet.** One meaning of **jet** is **stream of water or air.** Another meaning of the word is **airplane.**

3. Look at your worksheet for lesson 32. ✔
- You're going to look up each homograph in a dictionary, then write two different meanings for each one.
- Word A is **sock.** Look up **sock** in your dictionary. Raise your hand when you've found it.
- What's one meaning of the word **sock**? **(Idea:** *A covering for a foot; to hit or punch.*)
- Write that meaning of the word.
- What's another meaning of **sock**? **(Idea:** *To hit or punch; a covering for a foot.*)
- Write that meaning of the word **sock.**

4. Use your dictionary to find the meanings for the rest of the homographs. Write two meanings for each word. Raise your hand when you've finished.

5. (After the students complete the items, do a workcheck. For each item, call on a student to read the two meanings. If the answer is wrong, give the correct answer.)

Answer Key (Ideas): 1. a covering for the foot **2.** to hit or punch **3.** a kind of tree **4.** the inside of the hand **5.** in good health **6.** a hole dug for water **7.** not fat **8.** to slant **9.** strict **10.** the back of a ship

Lesson 33

HOMOGRAPHS

```
33
          Name _____
Lesson 33

Use your dictionary to find the meanings of the homographs. Write two
sentences for each word. Use a different meaning of the word in each
sentence.

A. top

1. _____

2. _____

B. yard

3. _____

4. _____

C. ring

5. _____

6. _____

D. present

7. _____

8. _____


178   BLM 33
```

1. Look at your worksheet for lesson 33. ✔
- You're going to use your dictionary to find the different meanings of the homographs. Then you're going to write a sentence for each meaning.
- Word A is **top.** One meaning of the word **top** is **a toy that spins.**
- Another meaning of the word **top** is **the highest point.**

2. Write two sentences, one using the word **top** to mean **a toy that spins,** and one using the word **top** to mean **the highest point.** Raise your hand when you're finished.
3. (Call on students to read aloud their sentences. If the sentences do not use words correctly, help students to correct them.)
4. Finish the items. For each homograph, write two sentences, each using a different meaning. Remember to use your dictionary.
5. (After the students complete the items, do a workcheck. For each item, call on a student to read the sentences. If a sentence uses a word incorrectly, give the correct use for the word.)

Answer Key: Answers will vary. Accept all sentences that use the correct meanings of the words.

Materials: Each student will need a copy of the worksheet for lesson 34 (Blackline Master 34); the teacher and each student will need a copy of the same children's dictionary.

Name _____
Lesson 34

Write a sentence for each homophone in a set. Use your dictionary.

1. board _____
_____

2. bored _____
_____

3. feat _____
_____

4. feet _____
_____

5. grate _____
_____

6. great _____
_____

7. cereal _____
_____

8. serial _____
_____

Copyright © by SRA/McGraw-Hill. Permission is granted to reproduce this page for classroom use.

BLM 34 179

1. What's the name for words that are spelled the same but have different meanings? (Signal.) *Homographs.*
2. Other words sound the same, but are spelled differently and have different meanings. The name for these words is **homophones.**
   - What's the name for words that sound the same but are spelled differently and have different meanings? (Signal.) *Homophones.*
3. Here are some homophones. (Write on the board:)

> 1. **sea, see**
> 2. **right, write**

4. Look at the first set of words: **sea** and **see.**
   - The word spelled **s-e-a** means **a large body of water.**

- The word spelled **s-e-e** means **to view.**
5. Look at the second set of words: **right** and **write.**
   - The word spelled **r-i-g-h-t** means **correct.**
   - The word spelled **w-r-i-t-e** means **to compose.**
6. Look at your worksheet for lesson 34. ✔
   - You're going to write a sentence for each of the homophones in a set. Use your dictionary to make sure you use the correct spelling.
7. The first set of words is **board** and **bored.**
   - What's the meaning of the word **board?** Look it up. (Idea: *A piece of lumber.*)
   - Write a sentence that uses **board.** Raise your hand when you've finished.
   - (Call on students to read their sentences. Accept only sentences that use the word correctly.)
   - What's the meaning of the word **bored?** Look it up. (Idea: *Not interested.*)
   - Write a sentence that uses **bored.** Raise your hand when you've finished.
   - (Call on students to read their sentences. Accept only sentences that use the word correctly.)
8. Write sentences for the rest of the homophones. Use your dictionary.
9. (After the students complete the items, do a workcheck. For each item, call on a student to read the sentences. If a sentence uses a word incorrectly, give the correct word.)

Answer Key: Answers will vary. Accept sentences that use the correct words.

Lesson 35

HOMOPHONES

35

Lesson 35

Name _____

Write a sentence for each homophone in a set. Use your dictionary.

1. cell _____
2. sell _____
3. fair _____
4. fare _____
5. dew _____
6. due _____
7. loan _____
8. lone _____

Copyright © by SRA/McGraw-Hill. Permission is granted to reproduce this page for classroom use.

180 BLM 35

1. What's the name for words that sound the same but are spelled differently and have different meanings? (Signal.) *Homophones.*
2. Here are some more homophones.
- (Write on the board:)

> 1. **coarse, course**
> 2. **buy, by**

- Look at the first set of words. The words **coarse** and **course** sound the same, but they are spelled differently and have different meanings.
- The word spelled **c-o-a-r-s-e** means **rough.**
- The word spelled **c-o-u-r-s-e** means **a school subject** or **a path.**

- Look at the second set of words. The word spelled **b-u-y** means **purchase.**
- The word spelled **b-y** means **near.**
3. Look at your worksheet for lesson 35. ✔
- You're going to write a sentence for each of the homophones in a set. Use your dictionary to make sure you use the correct spelling.
4. The first set of words is **cell** and **sell.**
- What's the meaning of the word **cell**? Look it up. (Ideas: *A small room; a prison room; a kind of phone.*)
- Write a sentence that uses **cell.** Raise your hand when you've finished.
- (Call on students to read their sentences. Accept sentences that use the word correctly.)
- What's the meaning of the word **sell**? Look it up. (Idea: *To exchange something for money.*)
- Write a sentence that uses **sell.** Raise your hand when you've finished.
- (Call on students to read their sentences. Accept sentences that use the word correctly.)
5. Write sentences for the rest of the homophones. Remember to use your dictionary.
6. (After the students complete the items, do a workcheck. For each item, call on a student to read the sentences. If a sentence uses a word incorrectly, give the correct word.)

Answer Key: Answers will vary. Accept sentences that use the correct words.

Materials: Each student will need a copy of the worksheet for lesson 36 (Blackline Master 36); the teacher and each student will need a copy of the same children's dictionary.

HOMOPHONES

```
                                              36
Name _____
Lesson 36

Write a sentence for each homophone in a set. Use your dictionary.

1. principal _____
              _____

2. principle _____
              _____

3. hair       _____
              _____

4. hare       _____
              _____

5. oar        _____
              _____

6. ore        _____
              _____

7. plain      _____
              _____

8. plane      _____
              _____

                                       BLM 36   181
```

1. What's the name for words that sound the same but are spelled differently and have different meanings? (Signal.) *Homophones.*
2. Look at your worksheet for lesson 36. ✔
• Write a sentence for each of the homophones in a set. Use your dictionary to make sure you use the correct spelling.

3. The first set of words is **principal** and **principle.**
• What's the meaning of the word **principal**? Look it up. (Idea: *The chief person or thing; the head of a school.*)
• Write a sentence that uses **principal.** Raise your hand when you've finished.
• (Call on students to read their sentences. Accept sentences that use the word correctly.)
• What's the meaning of the word **principle**? Look it up. (Ideas: *A rule; a belief; an ideal.*)
• Write a sentence that uses **principle.** Raise your hand when you've finished.
• (Call on students to read their sentences. Accept sentences that use the word correctly.)
4. Finish the items.
5. (After the students complete the items, do a workcheck. For each item, call on a student to read the sentences. If a sentence uses a word incorrectly, give the correct word.)

Answer Key: Answers will vary. Accept sentences that use the correct words

Lesson 37

Materials: Each student will need a copy of the worksheet for lesson 37 (Blackline Master 37).

CAPITALIZATION

37

Lesson 37

Name _____

• Begin the first word of every sentence with a capital letter.
• Begin the names of people, ethnic groups, places, organizations, languages, religions, and nationalities with capital letters.

If a word should begin with a capital letter, underline the letter.

1. please don't interrupt the speaker.
2. Our new neighbors are jeb and patsy ryan.
3. Michelle is french, but she speaks italian and english.
4. The new german teacher is from mobile, alabama.
5. the organization for applied technology held its meeting in freeport, maine, this year.
6. our library has a large collection of native american literature.

182 BLM 37

1. Look at your worksheet for lesson 37. ✔
• The box contains some rules about when to use capital letters.
• Follow along as I read what it says:

• Begin the first word of a sentence with a capital letter.
• Begin the names of people, ethnic groups, places, organizations, languages, religions, and nationalities with capital letters.

---

2. Item 1: please don't interrupt the speaker. What's wrong with the sentence? (Idea: *The first word doesn't begin with a capital letter.*)
• Write the sentence to make it correct.

• Item 2: Our new neighbors are jeb and patsy ryan. What's wrong with the sentence? (Idea: *The names **jeb, patsy, and ryan** don't begin with capital letters.*)
• Write the sentence to make it correct.
3. Do the rest of the items. If a word should begin with a capital letter, underline the letter. Raise your hand when you've finished.
4. (After the students complete the items, do a workcheck. For each item, call on a student to read the sentence. Have the student tell the words that should be capitalized and why. If the answer is wrong, give the correct answer.)

Answer Key:
1. <u>p</u>lease don't interrupt the speaker.
2. Our new neighbors are <u>j</u>eb and <u>p</u>atsy <u>r</u>yan.
3. Michelle is <u>f</u>rench, but she speaks <u>i</u>talian and <u>e</u>nglish.
4. The new german teacher is from <u>m</u>obile, <u>a</u>labama.
5. <u>t</u>he <u>o</u>rganization for <u>a</u>pplied <u>t</u>echnology held its meeting in <u>f</u>reeport, <u>m</u>aine, this year.
6. <u>o</u>ur library has a large collection of <u>n</u>ative <u>a</u>merican literature.

Lesson 38

Materials: Each student will need a copy of the worksheet for lesson 38 (Blackline Master 38).

CAPITALIZATION

> **38**
>
> Name _____
> **Lesson 38**
>
> - Begin the names of the days of the week with capital letters.
> - Begin the names of months with capital letters.
> - **Don't** begin the names of the seasons with capital letters.
> - **Don't** begin the names of words used to show directions with capital letters.
>
> **If a sentence doesn't use capital letters correctly, rewrite it. If it uses capital letters correctly, write correct.**
>
> 1. Mitch visits his friend every tuesday.
> _____
> 2. We usually take our vacation in june.
> _____
> 3. Each Spring, we plant new trees.
> _____
> 4. Colorado is North of New Mexico and West of Kansas.
> _____
> 5. Molly, Jeb, and Cindy were all born in April.
> _____
>
> BLM 38   183

1. Look at your worksheet for lesson 38. ✔
- The box contains some more rules about when to use capital letters.
- Follow along as I read what it says:

> - **Begin the names of the days of the week with capital letters.**
> - **Begin the names of months with capital letters.**
> - **Don't begin the names of the seasons with capital letters.**
> - **Don't begin the names of words used to show directions with capital letters.**

2. Item 1: **Mitch visits his friend every tuesday.** What's wrong with the sentence? **(Idea:** *The name of the weekday doesn't begin with a capital letter.*)

- Write the sentence to make it correct.
3. Item 2: **We usually take our vacation in june.**
- What's wrong with the sentence? **(Idea:** *The name of the month doesn't begin with a capital letter.*)
- Write the sentence to make it correct.
4. Item 3: **Each Spring, we plant new trees.** What's wrong with the sentence? **(Idea:** *Spring* *shouldn't begin with a capital letter.*)
- Write the sentence to make it correct.
5. Read the rest of the sentences. If a sentence doesn't use capital letters correctly, rewrite it. If it uses capital letters correctly, don't rewrite it. Raise your hand when you've finished.
6. (After the students complete the items, do a workcheck. For each item, call on a student to read the sentence. Have the student tell the words that should or should not be capitalized and why. If the answer is wrong, give the correct answer.)

Answer Key:
1. Mitch visits his friend every Tuesday.
2. We usually take our vacation in June.
3. Each spring, we plant new trees.
4. Colorado is north of New Mexico and west of Kansas.
5. (correct)

Lesson 39

Materials: Each student will need a copy of the worksheet for lesson 39 (Blackline Master 39).

CAPITALIZATION

39

Lesson 39

Name _____

If a sentence doesn't use capital letters correctly, rewrite it. If it uses capital letters correctly, write **correct.**

1. Corrina lives just south of the county line.

   _____

2. do you know the way to san jose?

   _____

3. I can't remember if your birthday is in march or april.

   _____

4. larry is a member of scientists for the public interest.

   _____

5. The program was supported by Catholics, Jews, and Muslims.

   _____

6. Martin is african american, and kim is asian american.

   _____

7. my favorite time of year is winter.

   _____

184 BLM 39

1. Let's review some rules about when to use capital letters:
- Begin the first word of a sentence with a capital letter.
- Begin the names of people, ethnic groups, places, organizations, languages, religions, and nationalities with capital letters.
- Begin the names of days of the week with capital letters.
- Begin the names of months with capital letters.
- **Don't** begin the names of the seasons with capital letters.
- **Don't** begin the names of words used to show directions with capital letters.

2. Look at your worksheet for lesson 39. ✔
- Rewrite each sentence using capital letters correctly. If a sentence uses capital letters correctly, don't rewrite it. Raise your hand when you've finished.

3. (After the students complete the items, do a workcheck. For each item, call on a student to read the sentence. Have the student tell the words that should or should not be capitalized and why. If the answer is wrong, give the correct answer.)

Answer Key:
1. (correct)
2. Do you know the way to San Jose?
3. I can't remember if your birthday is in March or April.
4. Larry is a member of Scientists for the Public Interest.
5. (correct)
6. Martin is African American, and Kim is Asian American.
7. My favorite time of year is winter.

COMPLETE SENTENCES

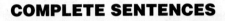

> 40
>
> Name _____
> **Lesson 40**
>
> **If Sean says a complete sentence, don't rewrite it. If he says a fragment, write a complete sentence.**
>
> 1. **Mandy:** Did you go to the baseball game or to the movies last Saturday?
>   **Sean:** Baseball game.
>   _____
>
> 2. **Mandy:** Was it a good game?
>   **Sean:** Pretty good.
>   _____
>
> 3. **Mandy:** Are you going to the game next Saturday?
>   **Sean:** I wouldn't miss it.
>   _____
>
> 4. **Mandy:** Whom are we playing?
>   **Sean:** Blazers.
>   _____
>
> 5. **Mandy:** I'd like to go to the game with you.
>   **Sean:** That's a great idea.
>   _____
>
> 6. **Mandy:** Should I meet you at the ticket office or the bus stop?
>   **Sean:** Ticket office.
>   _____
>
> BLM 40 **185**

1. A **sentence** is a group of words that expresses a complete thought. A group of words that doesn't express a complete thought is called a **sentence fragment.** A sentence begins with a capital letter and ends with a punctuation mark.

• What is a sentence? (Idea: *A group of words that expresses a complete thought.*)

• What is a sentence fragment? (Idea: *A group of words that doesn't express a complete thought.*)

2. Look at your worksheet for lesson 40. ✔

• This is a conversation between Mandy and Sean. Follow along as I read:

3. Item 1: **Mandy: Did you go to the baseball game or to the movies last Saturday afternoon? Sean: Baseball game.**

• Did Mandy express a complete thought to Sean? (Signal.) *Yes.*

• Yes, so what she said is a sentence.

• Did Sean's answer express a complete thought? (Signal.) *No.*

• No, so what he said is a sentence fragment.

• Write what Sean could have said to make his answer a sentence. Look at what Mandy said to find the words to use.
  (Observe students and give feedback.)

• (Write on the board:)

> 1. **I went to the baseball game.**

• Here's what you should have written for Item 1.

4. Item 2: **Mandy: Was it a good game**? **Sean: Pretty good.**

• Did Mandy express a complete thought? (Signal.) *Yes.*

• Did Sean answer Mandy with a complete thought? (Signal.) *No.*

• Write what Sean could have said to make his answer a sentence.
  (Observe students and give feedback.)

• (Write on the board:)

> 2. **It was a pretty good game.**

• Here's what you should have written for Item 2.

5. Read the rest of the conversation. If Sean says a complete sentence, don't rewrite it. If he says a fragment, write a complete sentence.
  (Observe students and give feedback.)

6. Check your work.

7. Item 3: **Mandy: Are you going to the game next Saturday? Sean: I wouldn't miss it.**
- Is Sean's answer a sentence? (Signal.) *Yes.*

8. Item 4: **Mandy: Who are we playing? Sean: Blazers.**
- Is Sean's answer a sentence? (Signal.) *No.*
- What sentence did you write? (Idea: *We're playing the Blazers.*)

9. Item 5: **Mandy: I'd like to go to the game with you. Sean: That's a great idea.**
- Is Sean's response a sentence? (Signal.) *Yes.*

10. Item 6: **Mandy: Should I meet you at the ticket office or the bus stop? Sean: Ticket office.**
- Is Sean's reply a sentence? (Signal.) *No.*
- What sentence did you write? (Ideas: *Meet me at the ticket office; you should meet me at the ticket office.*)

11. Raise your hand if you wrote sentences only for items **1, 2, 4,** and **6.**

COMPLETE SENTENCES

> **41**
>
> Name _____
>
> Lesson 41
>
> If an item is a fragment, rewrite it as a sentence. If it is a sentence, write correct.
>
> 1. Over the mountains.
>
>   _____
>
> 2. I plan to spend the summer swimming and riding my scooter.
>
>   _____
>
> 3. Bright stars filled the sky.
>
>   _____
>
> 4. A large piece of cake.
>
>   _____
>
> 5. An unusual place.
>
>   _____
>
> 6. Tadpoles live in our pond.
>
>   _____
>
> 7. Once a week.
>
>   _____
>
> 8. Please call when you have time.
>
>   _____
>
> 186 BLM 41

1. Let's review what you've learned about sentences.
- A **sentence** is a group of words that tells a complete thought.
- A group of words that doesn't tell a complete thought is called a **sentence fragment.**
- A sentence begins with a capital letter and ends with a punctuation mark.

2. Look at your worksheet for lesson 41. ✔
- If an item is a fragment, rewrite it as a sentence. If it is a sentence, don't write anything.
3. Item 1: **Over the mountains.**
- Is that a sentence? (Signal.) *No.*
- Rewrite it as a sentence.
- (Call on students to read their sentences. Accept complete sentences.)
4. Item 2: **I plan to spend the summer swimming and riding my scooter.**
- Is that a sentence? (Signal.) *Yes.*
- Don't rewrite it.
5. Finish the items. Raise your hand when you've finished.
6. Item 3: **Bright stars filled the sky.**
- Is that a sentence? (Signal.) *Yes.*
7. Item 4: **A large piece of cake.**
- Is that a sentence? (Signal.) *No.*
- What sentence did you write? (Accept complete sentences.)
8. (Repeat for the remaining items.)
9. Raise you hand if you wrote sentences for items **1, 4, 5,** and **7.**

Lesson 42

Materials: Each student will need a copy of the worksheet for lesson 42 (Blackline Master 42).

COMPLETE SUBJECTS AND PREDICATES

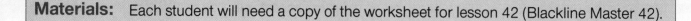

Name _____
Lesson 42

Circle the subject and underline the predicate.

1. Paulo plays tennis.

2. Paulo and Steve play tennis often.

3. Paulo and his friends play tennis in the park.

4. Beth's little sister likes to play video games.

5. The angry crowd marched to the state capitol.

6. Some people in the crowd shouted and jeered.

7. The leading race car crashed into a wall.

8. Uncle Fred and Aunt Colleen came for a visit last week.

9. The children and their parents applauded the smiling principal.

10. Dennis, Harry, and Kyle decided to form a ska band.

BLM 42 187

1. Complete sentences have two main parts: the **subject** and the **predicate.**
2. The **subject** is the part of a sentence that tells whom or what the sentence is about. The **predicate** is the part of the sentence that tells what the subject is, does, or is like.
- What are the two main parts of a sentence. (Signal.) *Subject and predicate.*
- Which part tells whom or what the sentence is about? (Signal.) *The subject.*
- Which part tells what the subject is, does, or is like? (Signal.) *The predicate.*
3. Look at your worksheet for lesson 42. ✔
4. Sentence 1 is **Paulo plays tennis.**
- What's the subject? (Signal.) *Paulo.*
- What's the predicate? (Signal.) *Plays tennis.*

5. Sentence 2: **Paulo and Steve play tennis often.**
- What's the subject? (Idea: *Paulo and Steve.*)
- What's the predicate? (Idea: *Play tennis often.*)
6. Sentence 3: **Paulo and his friends play tennis in the park.**
- What's the subject? (Idea: *Paulo and his friends.*)
- What's the predicate? (Idea: *Play tennis in the park.*)
7. Read the rest of the sentences. Circle the subject and underline the predicate in each sentence. Raise your hand when you've finished.
8. (After the students complete the items, do a workcheck. For each item, call on a student to read the sentence. Have the student say the words circled and the words underlined. If the answer is wrong, give the correct answer.)

Answer Key:
1. (Paulo) plays tennis.
2. (Paulo and Steve) play tennis often.
3. (Paulo and his friends) play tennis in the park.
4. (Beth's little sister) likes to play video games.
5. (The angry crowd) marched to the state capitol.
6. (Some people in the crowd) shouted and jeered.
7. (The leading race car) crashed into a wall.
8. (Uncle Fred and Aunt Colleen) came for a visit last week.
9. (The children and their parents) applauded the smiling principal.
10. (Dennis, Harry, and Kyle) decided to form a ska band.

Materials: Each student will need a copy of the worksheet for lesson 43 (Blackline Master 43).

COMPLETE SUBJECTS AND PREDICATES

> **43**
>
> Lesson 43
>
> Name ——————————————
>
> Circle the subject and underline the predicate in each sentence.
>
> 1. Sylvia created her own Web page.
>
> 2. My cousin Sylvia created her own Web page as a class project.
>
> 3. Ms. Colson teaches geometry and algebra.
>
> 4. The New York Yankees won the World Series in 2000.
>
> 5. A large red truck roared past us on the narrow road.
>
> 6. This unusual painting shows seven different views of the Japanese mountain.
>
> 7. Our French class wrote letters to students in Paris.
>
> 8. The raging floodwaters reached the second floor of our house.
>
> 9. Five happy puppies frolicked and tumbled in the grass.
>
> 10. Everybody in the group agreed to donate time to the project.
>
> 188 BLM 43

1. Let's review what you've learned about subjects and predicates.
- The **subject** is the part of the sentence that tells whom or what the sentence is about.
- The **predicate** is the part of the sentence that tells what the subject is, does, or is like.
2. Look at your worksheet for lesson 43. ✔
- Sentence 1. **Sylvia created her own Web page.**
- What's the subject? (Signal.) *Sylvia.*
- What's the predicate? (Signal.) *Created her own Web page.*
3. Sentence 2: **My cousin Sylvia created her own Web page as a class project.**
- What's the subject? (Signal.) *My cousin Sylvia.*

- What's the predicate? (Signal.) *Created her own Web page as a class project.*
4. Read the rest of the sentences. Circle the subject and underline the predicate in each sentence.
5. (After the students complete the items, do a workcheck. For each item, call on a student to read the sentence. Have the student say the words circled and the words underlined. If the answer is wrong, give the correct answer.)

Answer Key:
1. (Sylvia) created her own Web page.
2. (My cousin Sylvia) created her own Web page as a class project.
3. (Ms. Colson) teaches geometry and algebra.
4. (The New York Yankees) won the World Series in 2000.
5. (A large red truck) roared past us on the narrow road.
6. (This unusual painting) shows seven different views of the Japanese mountain.
7. (Our French class) wrote letters to students in Paris.
8. (The raging floodwaters) reached the second floor of our house.
9. (Five happy puppies) frolicked and tumbled in the grass.
10. (Everybody in the group) agreed to donate time to the project.

Lesson 44

Materials: Each student will need a copy of the worksheet for lesson 44 (Blackline Master 44).

NOUNS

Name _____

Lesson 44

44

- A **noun** is a word that names a person, place, thing, idea, or feeling.

Circle the words that can be nouns. Cross out the words that do not name people, places, things, ideas, or feelings.

1. sadly

2. Luke

3. lonely

4. house

5. Kansas

6. Supreme Court

7. tree

8. laugh

BLM 44   189

1. Sentences are made up of words called **parts of speech.** If you can identify what part of speech a word is, you can figure out the role the word plays in a sentence.

- A **noun** is one part of speech.

2. Look at your worksheet for lesson 44. ✔

- The box contains some information about nouns. Follow along as I read what it says:

> A **noun** is a word that names a person, place, thing, idea, or feeling.

- What's a noun? (Idea: *A word that names a person, place, thing, idea, or feeling.*)

3. Circle the words that can be nouns. Cross out the words that cannot be nouns.

- Item 1: **sadly.** Does it name a person, place, thing, idea, or feeling? (Signal.) *No.*

- **Sadly** isn't a noun. Don't circle it.

- Item 2: **Luke.** Does it name a person, place, thing, idea, or feeling? (Signal.) *Yes.*

- Yes, **Luke** is a person's name, so it's a noun. Circle it.

4. Finish the items. Raise your hand when you've finished.

5. Check your work.

6. Item 3: **lonely.**

- Is that a noun? (Signal.) *No.*

7. Item 4: **house.**

- Is that a noun? (Signal.) *Yes.*

8. (Repeat for the remaining items.)

Lesson 45

Materials: Each student will need a copy of the worksheet for lesson 45 (Blackline Master 45).

COMMON AND PROPER NOUNS

> **45**
> Lesson 45
> Name _____
>
> • A **common** noun is a word that names *any* person, place, thing, idea, or feeling.
> • A **proper** noun names a *particular* person, place, thing, idea, or feeling. Proper nouns always begin with a capital letter.
>
> Write **common** if a word is a common noun and **proper** if it is a proper noun.
>
> 1. Paula _____
> 2. shovel _____
> 3. Detroit _____
> 4. water _____
> 5. saddle _____
> 6. cave _____
> 7. events _____
> 8. Abigail _____
> 9. bridge _____
> 10. Statue of Liberty _____
> 11. sister _____
> 12. Iran _____
>
> 190   BLM 45

1. What's a noun? (Idea: *A word that names a person, place, thing, idea, or feeling.*)
2. Look at your worksheet for lesson 45. ✔
- The box contains some more information about nouns. Follow along as I read:

> • A **common** noun is a word that names *any* person, place, thing, idea, or feeling.
> • A **proper** noun names a *particular* person, place, thing, idea, or feeling. Proper nouns always being with a capital letter.

- What's a common noun? (Idea: *A word that names **any** person, place, thing, idea, or feeling.*)
- What's a proper noun? (Idea: *A word that names a **particular** person, place, thing, idea, or feeling.*)
- The word **building** is a common noun, and **Pentagon** is a proper noun.
- The word **college** is a common noun. What's a proper noun for a college? (Accept appropriate answers.)
- **January** is a proper noun. What's a common noun for January? (Idea: *Month.*)
3. It's your turn. Write **common** if a word is a common noun and **proper** if it is a proper noun. Raise your hands when you're finished. (Observe students and give feedback.)
4. (After the students complete the items, do a workcheck. For each item, call on a student to tell whether the word is a noun and whether it is a common or proper noun. If the answer is wrong, give the correct answer.)

Answer Key:

1. proper	**7.** common
2. common	**8.** proper
3. proper	**9.** common
4. common	**10.** proper
5. common	**11.** common
6. common	**12.** proper

Lesson 45 49

Lesson 46

SINGULAR AND PLURAL NOUNS

Name _____
Lesson 46   46

- A **singular** noun names one person, place, thing, idea, or feeling.
- A **plural** noun names more than one.
- Most nouns are made plural by adding **s**.
- Nouns that end with **s, z, ch, sh,** and **x** are made plural by adding **es**.

A. I. the noun names one person, place, thing, idea, or feeling, write **singular**. If it names more than one, write **plural**.

1. rabbits   _____
2. coat   _____
3. cabbage   _____
4. bushes   _____
5. foxes   _____

B. Write the plural of each noun.

1. bus   _____
2. trumpet   _____
3. kiss   _____
4. church   _____
5. friend   _____

BLM 46   191

1. Look at your worksheet for lesson 46. ✔
- The box contains more information about nouns. Follow along as I read:

> - A **singular** noun names one person, place, thing, idea, or feeling.
> - A **plural** noun names more than one.
> - Most nouns are made plural by adding **s**.
> - Nouns that end with **s, z, ch, sh,** and **x** are made plural by adding **es**.

2. Look at part A on your worksheet. ✔
If the noun names one person, place, thing, idea, or feeling, write **singular**. If it names more than one, write **plural**.
- Item 1 is **rabbits.** It that a singular or plural noun? (Signal.) *Plural.*
- Yes. **Rabbits** names more than one rabbit.
- Item 2 is **coat.** Is that singular or plural? (Signal.) *Singular.*
- Finish the items in part A. Raise your hand when you've finished.
(Observe students and give feedback.)
3. Now look at part B. ✔
- Write the plural of each noun. Raise your hand when you've finished.
(Observe students and give feedback.)
4. (After the students complete the items in both parts, do a workcheck. For each item in part A, call on a student to tell whether the noun is singular or plural. For part B, call on a student to spell the plural of each word. If an answer is wrong, give the correct answer.)

Answer Key: Part A: 1. plural **2.** singular **3.** singular **4.** plural **5.** plural
Part B: 1. buses **2.** trumpets **3.** kisses **4.** churches **5.** friends

Materials: Each student will need a copy of the worksheet for lesson 47 (Blackline Master 47).

PLURAL NOUNS

47

Lesson 47

Name _____

- Nouns that end with a consonant followed by **y** are made plural by changing the y to **i** and adding **es.**
- Nouns that end with a vowel followed by **y** are made plural by adding s.
- Nouns that end with **f** are made plural by changing the f to v and adding es.

Write the plural of each noun.

1. leaf _____
2. city _____
3. day _____
4. country _____
5. self _____
6. turkey _____
7. loaf _____
8. thief _____
9. play _____

192 BLM 47

1. Look at your worksheet for lesson 47. ✔
- The box contains more information about plural nouns. Follow along as I read:

> - Nouns that end with a consonant followed by **y** are made plural by changing the **y** to **i** and adding **es.**
> - Nouns that end with a vowel followed by **y** are made plural by adding **s.**
> - Nouns that end with **f** are made plural by changing the **f** to **v** and adding **es.**

2. Look at your worksheet. ✔
   Write the plural of each noun.
- Item 1 is **leaf.** How do you make it plural? (Idea: *Change the **f** to **v** and add **es.***)
- The plural for **leaf** is **l-e-a-v-e-s.** Write it down.
- Item 2 is **city. City** ends with a consonant followed by **y.** How do you make it plural? (Idea: *Change the **y** to **i** and add **es.***)
- Yes. The plural for **city** is **c-i-t-i-e-s.** Write it down.
- Item 3 is **day. Day** ends with a vowel followed by **y.** How do you make it plural? (Idea: *Add **s.***)
- Yes. Don't change the spelling, just add **s.** The plural for **day** is **d-a-y-s.** Write it down.
- Do the rest of the items. Raise your hand when you've finished.
   (Observe students and give feedback.)
3. (After the students complete the items, do a workcheck. For each item, call on a student to spell the plural. If an answer is wrong, give the correct answer.)

Answer Key: 1. leaves **2.** cities **3.** days **4.** countries **5.** selves **6.** turkeys **7.** loaves **8.** thieves **9.** plays

Lesson 48

IRREGULAR PLURAL NOUNS

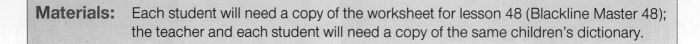

Name _____
Lesson 48

48

- Some nouns have **irregular** plural forms.
- You can't predict how to make the plural form of an irregular noun. Sometimes you have to check its spelling in a dictionary.

Write the plural of each noun. Use your dictionary.

1. medium   _____
2. oasis   _____
3. child   _____
4. foot   _____
5. series   _____
6. mouse   _____
7. sheep   _____
8. woman   _____

Copyright © by SRA/McGraw-Hill. Permission is granted to reproduce this page for classroom use.

BLM 48 193

1. Look at your worksheet for lesson 48. ✔
- The box contains some more information about plural nouns. Follow along as I read:

> - Some nouns have **irregular** plural forms.
> - You can't predict how to make the plural form of an irregular noun. Sometimes you have to check its spelling in a dictionary.

2. Look at your worksheet. ✔
   Write the plural of each noun. Use your dictionary.
- Item 1 is **medium.** Look it up. What's the plural? (Idea: *Media.*)
- Item 2 is **oasis.** Look it up. What's the plural? (Idea: *Oases.*)
- Item 3 is **child.** You should already know the plural of **child.** What is it? (Idea: *Children.*)
- Do the rest of the items. Raise your hand when you've finished.
   (Observe students and give feedback.)
3. (After the students complete the items, do a workcheck. For each item, call on a student to spell the plural. If an answer is wrong, give the correct answer.)

Answer Key: 1. media **2.** oases **3.** children **4.** feet **5.** series **6.** mice **7.** sheep **8.** women

Materials: Each student will need a copy of the worksheet for lesson 49 (Blackline Master 49).

EXERCISE 1
POSSESSIVE NOUNS

49

Lesson 49

Name _____

- **Possessive** nouns tell who or what owns or has something.
- Most singular nouns are made possessive by adding an apostrophe (') and **s**.
- Most plural nouns ending in s are made possessive by adding an apostrophe (').

A. Write **S** if the noun is singular and **P** if it is plural. Then write the possessive form.

	Singular/Plural	Possessive
1. Dana		
2. babies		
3. wolves		
4. Lois		

B. Write the plural of each noun.

1. box	5. goose	
2. calf	6. bench	
3. key	7. team	
4. wheat	8. cherry	

194 BLM 49

1. Look at your worksheet for lesson 49. ✔
- The box contains more information about nouns. Follow along as I read:

> - **Possessive** nouns tell who or what owns or has something.
> - Most singular nouns are made possessive by adding an **apostrophe** (') and **s**.
> - Most plural nouns ending in **s** are made possessive by adding an **apostrophe** (').

- What's the name for a noun that tells who or what owns something? (Signal.) *Possessive.*

- How do you make most singular nouns possessive? (Idea: *Add an apostrophe and s.*)
- How do you make most plural nouns possessive? (Idea: *Add an apostrophe.*)
2. Look at part A on your worksheet. ✔ If the noun is singular, write **S**. If it is plural, write **P**. Then write the possessive form.
- Item 1: **Dana.** Is that singular or plural? (Signal.) *Singular.*
- How do you make **Dana** possessive? (Idea: *Add an apostrophe and s.*)
- Yes. The possessive for **Dana** is **Dana's.** Write the answer.
- Item 2 is **babies.** Is that singular or plural? (Signal.) *Plural.*
- How do you make it possessive? (Idea: *Add an apostrophe.*)
- That's right. **Babies** is plural, so you just add an apostrophe. Write the answer.
- Finish the items in part A. (Observe students and give feedback.)
3. (After the students complete the items, do a workcheck. For each item, call on a student to tell whether the noun is singular or plural and spell the possessive. If an answer is wrong, give the correct answer.)

Answer Key: Part A: 1. S, Dana's
2. P, babies' **3.** P, wolves' **4.** S, Lois's

EXERCISE 2

PLURAL NOUNS

1. Let's review what you've learned about plural nouns.
- How do you make most nouns plural? (Idea: *By adding* **s**.)
- How do you make nouns that end with **s, z, ch, sh,** and **x** plural? (Idea: *By adding* **es.**)
- How do you make a noun that ends in **f** plural? (Idea: *Change the* **f** *to* **v** *and add* **es.**)
- How do you make a noun that ends with a consonant followed by **y** plural? (Idea: *Change the* **y** *to* **i** *and add* **es.**)
- How do you make a noun that ends with a vowel followed by **y** plural? (Idea: *Add* **s.**)
- How do you figure out irregular plurals? (Idea: *Use a dictionary.*)

2. Look at part B on your worksheet. ✔
- Write the plural of each of the nouns. Raise your hand when you've finished. **(Observe students and give feedback.)**
3. (Write on the board:)

1.	**boxes**	5.	**geese**
2.	**calves**	6.	**benches**
3.	**keys**	7.	**teams**
4.	**wheat**	8.	**cherries**

4. Here's what you should have. Correct any mistakes.

Lesson 50

POSSESSIVE NOUNS

Name _____
Lesson 50

Write the singular and plural possessive.

	Singular Possessive	Plural Possessive
1. tax		
2. elf		
3. dish		
4. journey		
5. desk		
6. candy		
7. waltz		
8. home		

50

BLM 50 195

Copyright © by SRA/McGraw-Hill. Permission is granted to reproduce this page for classroom use.

1. What's the name for a noun that tells who or what owns something? (Signal.) *Possessive.*
   - How do you make most singular nouns possessive? (Idea: *Add an apostrophe and* **s.**)
   - How do you make most plural nouns possessive? (Idea: *Add an apostrophe.*)
2. Look at your worksheet for lesson 50. ✔
   - Write the singular and plural possessive of each noun.

- Item 1 is **tax.** How do you make it possessive? (Idea: *Add an apostrophe and* **s.**)
- How do you make **tax** plural? (Idea: *Add* **es.**)
- How do you make **taxes** possessive? (Idea: *Add an apostrophe.*)
- Item 2 is **elf.** How do you make it possessive? (Idea: *Add an apostrophe and* **s.**)
- How do you make **elf** plural? (Idea: *Change the* **f** *to* **v** *and add* **es.**)
- How do you make **elves** possessive? (Idea: *Add an apostrophe.*)
- Finish the items. Raise your hand when you've finished.
   (Observe students and give feedback.)
3. (Write on the board:)

1. **tax's, taxes'**	6. **candy's,**
2. **elf's, elves'**	**candies'**
3. **dish's, dishes'**	7. **waltz's,**
4. **journey's,**	**waltzes'**
journeys'	8. **home's,**
5. **desk's, desks'**	**homes'**

4. Here's what you should have. Correct any mistakes.

Lesson 51

PRONOUNS

51

Lesson 51

Name _____

- **Pronouns** are words that take the place of nouns.
- **Personal pronouns** refer to people or things.
- Here are some personal pronouns: **I, me, you, he, him, she, her, it, we, us, they, them.**

Circle the pronouns in each sentence.

1. I like to go to movies.

2. The firefighter praised us for acting quickly.

3. Did they give it to him or to her?

4. Please tell me a story.

5. He called them early in the morning.

6. She and Shaunna belong to a book club.

7. Where is he staying?

8. Can we go with you to the zoo?

Copyright © by SRA/McGraw-Hill. Permission is granted to reproduce this page for classroom use.

196   BLM 51

---

1. You're going to learn about another part of speech, **pronouns.**
2. Look at your worksheet for lesson 51. ✔
- The box contains some information about pronouns. Follow along as I read:

- **Pronouns** are words that take the place of nouns.
- **Personal pronouns** refer to people or things.
- Here are some personal pronouns: **I, me, you, he, him, she, her, it, we, us, they, them.**

- What are pronouns? (Idea: *Words that take the place of nouns.*)
- What are personal pronouns? (Idea: *Pronouns that refer to people or things.*)
- For the noun **children,** the personal pronouns are **they** and **them.**

- For the noun **video,** the personal pronoun is **it.**
- What are the personal pronouns for the noun **Sharon**? (Ideas: *She and her.*)
- What are the personal pronouns for the noun **father**? (Ideas: *He and him.*)
3. Circle the pronouns in each sentence.
- Item 1: **I like to go to movies.** What's the pronoun? (Signal.) *I.*
- That's right. Circle **I.**
- Item 2: **The firefighter praised us for acting quickly.** What's the pronoun? (Signal.) *Us.*
- Yes, circle **us.**
- Item 3: **Did they give it to him or to her?** What's the pronoun? (Signal.) *They.*
- What's another pronoun? (Signal.) *It.*
- What's another pronoun? (Signal.) *Him.*
- What's another pronoun? (Signal.) *Her.*
- So you circle four words: **they, it, him, and her.**
4. Do the rest of the items. Raise your hand when you've finished.
   (Observe students and give feedback.)
5. (After the students complete the items, do a workcheck. For each item, call on a student to give the pronouns in each sentence. If an answer is wrong, give the correct answer.)

Answer Key:
1. I like to go to movies.
2. The firefighter praised us for acting quickly.
3. Did they give it to him or to her?
4. Please tell me a story.
5. He called them early in the morning.
6. She and Shaunna belong to a book club.
7. Where is he staying?
8. Can we go with you to the zoo?

Materials: Each student will need a copy of the worksheet for lesson 52 (Blackline Master 52).

POSSESSIVE PRONOUNS

Name _____

Lesson 52

- **Possessive pronouns** are words that tell who or what owns something.
- Possessive pronouns can replace possessive nouns.
- Possessive pronouns **aren't** written with apostrophes.
- Here are some possessive pronouns: **my, mine, your, yours, her, hers, his, its, our, ours, their, theirs.**

Rewrite the sentences. Use possessive pronouns.

1. Laura's family is moving to Fairbanks.

2. Is this Ken's bike helmet, or is it Delia's?

3. That book belongs to me.

4. Rugby's rules are hard to understand.

5. Paula's house is on the same street as Mel's and Brad's.

6. Dolores's hobby is bird watching.

BLM 52 197

1. Look at your worksheet for lesson 52. ✔
- The box contains some more information about pronouns. Follow along as I read:

> - **Possessive pronouns** are words that tell who or what owns or has something.
> - Possessive pronouns can replace possessive nouns.
> - Possessive pronouns **aren't** written with apostrophes.
> - Here are some possessive pronouns: **my, mine, your, yours, her, hers, his, its, our, ours, their, theirs.**

2. What's the name for a pronoun that tells who or what owns or has something? (Signal.) *Possessive.*
3. Rewrite the sentences. Use possessive pronouns.
- Item 1: **Laura's family is moving to Fairbanks.** What's the sentence? (Idea: *Her family is moving to Fairbanks.*)
- Item 2: **Is this Ken's bike helmet, or is it Delia's?**
- What's the sentence? (Idea: *Is it his bike helmet, or is it hers?*)
- Item 3: **That book belongs to me.**
- What's the sentence? (Ideas: *The book is mine; It is my book.*)
4. Do the rest of the items. Raise your hand when you've finished.
(Observe students and give feedback.)
5. (After the students complete the items, do a workcheck. For each item, call on a student to read the rewritten sentence. If an answer is wrong, give the correct answer.)

Answer Key: (Ideas:)
1. Her family is moving to Fairbanks.
2. Is this his bike helmet, or is it hers?
3. The book is mine. **or** It is my book.
4. Its rules are hard to understand.
5. Her house is on the same street as theirs.
6. Her hobby is bird watching.

Lesson 53

Materials: Each student will need a copy of the worksheet for lesson 53 (Blackline Master 53).

PRONOUNS AND ANTECEDENTS

1. Look at your worksheet for lesson 53. ✔
- The box contains some more information about pronouns. Follow along as I read:

> - The word that a pronoun refers to is called an **antecedent.**
> - **Antecedent** means "a word that goes before."
> - When you write pronouns, make sure they refer clearly to their antecedents.

2. What's the name for a word that a pronoun refers to? (Signal.) *Antecedent.*
3. (Write on the board:)

> 1. **Joanne went to the museum yesterday. She had a good time.**
> 2. **Joanne went to see Teresa yesterday. She was sick.**

- Example 1: **Joanne went to the museum yesterday. She had a good time.**
- What's the pronoun? (Signal.) *She.*
- To what does **She** refer? (Idea: *Joanne.*)
- Yes, the pronoun **She** refers to **Joanne.** So **Joanne** is the antecedent of **She.**
- Example 2 is **Joanne went to see Teresa yesterday. She was sick.**
- What's the pronoun? (Signal.) *She.*
- But you can't tell which noun **She** refers to. The antecedent could be **Joanne** or it could be **Teresa.** The pronoun isn't clear. To make it clear who is sick, the second sentence needs to be rewritten: **Joanne went to see Teresa yesterday. Teresa was sick.**
4. It's your turn. If an item has a clear pronoun and antecedent, underline the pronoun and circle its antecedent. If a pronoun doesn't have a clear antecedent, rewrite the item to make it clear. Raise your hand when you've finished.

(Observe students and give feedback.)

4. (After the students complete the items, do a workcheck. For each item, call on a student to tell what is circled and underlined and to read any rewritten sentences. If an answer is wrong, give the correct answer.)

Answer Key:

1. (Ideas:) Phil went to the station with Joe. Phil caught the last train. **or** Phil went to the station with Joe. Joe caught the last train.

2. Mike bought new (sneakers). <u>They</u> are orange.

3. (Ideas:) Mike bought new sneakers for his brother. His brother likes orange. **or** Mike bought new sneakers for his brother. Mike likes orange.

4. Kent invited (Nancy) to join the chess club. <u>She</u> was thrilled!

5. (Sheila) told Patrick that <u>she</u> will take calculus next year.

6. Stan is interested in (physics). <u>It</u> is a difficult subject.

Lesson 54

Materials: Each student will need a copy of the worksheet for lesson 54 (Blackline Master 54).

VERBS

Name _____
Lesson 54

54

- Every sentence has a **verb.**
- Some verbs express the **action of a sentence.**
- Verbs can express physical actions: **walk, laugh, look.** They can also express mental actions: **think, plan, forget.**
- The words **has, have,** and **had** can be action verbs. They can be used alone or with other verbs.

A. Underline the verb in each sentence.

1. Tom remembered the appointment.
2. Tom has remembered the appointment.
3. Tom had an appointment.
4. Elephants live in India.
5. Elephants have trunks.
6. Inez has arrived in Chicago.

B. Write sentences for each verb.

1. march _____
2. have worn _____
3. memorize _____
4. has forgotten _____
5. disappear _____

BLM 54   199

1. You're going to learn about another part of speech: **verbs.**
2. Look at your worksheet for lesson 54. ✔
- I'll read what it says. Follow along:

> - Every sentence has a **verb.**
> - Some verbs express the **action** of a sentence.
> - Verbs can express physical actions: **walk, laugh, look.** They can also express mental actions: **think, plan, forget.**
> - The words **has, have,** and **had** can also be action verbs. They can be used alone or with other verbs. When they are used with other verbs, they are called **helping verbs.**

- What's the name for words that express actions in sentences? (Signal.) *Verbs.*
3. Find part A. Underline the verb in each sentence.
- Look at Item 1: **Tom remembered the appointment.**
- What's the verb? (Idea: *Remembered.*)
- Item 2: **Tom has remembered the appointment.**
- What's the verb? (Idea: *Has remembered.*)
- Item 3: **Tom had an appointment.**
- What's the verb? (Idea: *Had.*)
4. Do the rest of the items. Raise your hand when you've finished.
5. Check your work.
- Item 4 is **Elephants live in India.** You should have underlined **live.**
- Item 5: **Elephants have trunks.** You should have underlined **have.**
- Item 6: **Inez has arrived in Chicago.** You should have underlined **has arrived.**
- Correct any mistakes.
6. Find part B on your worksheet. ✔
- Write sentences for each verb. Raise your hand when you've finished. (Observe students and give feedback.)
7. (Call on students to read their sentences.)

Answer Key: (Part B:) Answers will vary. Accept correct sentences.

LINKING VERBS

55

Lesson 55

Name _____

- Linking verbs are words that connect words in the subject with words in the predicate in order to complete the meaning of a sentence.
- Here are some common linking verbs: **am, be, is, are, was, were, become.**

A. Underline the linking verb in each sentence.

1. The house is quiet.
2. The morning was hot and steamy.
3. The congressman became angry.
4. All the buses were empty.
5. My two grandmothers are friends.
6. I am late.

B. Write sentences for each linking verb.

1. to be _____
2. were _____
3. become _____
4. am _____
5. was _____

200   BLM 55

1. What's the name for words that express the actions in sentences? (Signal.) *Verbs.*
2. Look at your worksheet for lesson 55. ✔
- Here's some more information about verbs. Follow along as I read what's in the box:

> - **Linking verbs** are words that connect words in the subject with words in the predicate in order to complete the meaning of a sentence.
> - Here are some common linking verbs: **am, be, is, are, was, were, become.**

- What's the name for verbs such as **am, is, are,** and **were**? (Signal.) *Linking verbs.*
- What do linking verbs do? (Idea: *Link words in the subject to words in the predicate.*)

3. Find part A. Underline the linking verb in each sentence.
- Item 1: **The house is quiet.**
- What's the linking verb? (Idea: *Is.*)
- Yes. **Is** links the subject word **house** with the predicate word **quiet** to complete the meaning of the sentence.
- Item 2: **The morning was hot and steamy.**
- What's the verb? (Idea: *Was.*)
- Item 3: **The congressman became angry.**
- What's the verb? (Idea: *Became.*)
4. Do the rest of the items. Raise your hand when you've finished.
5. Check your work.
- Item 4: **All the buses were empty.** You should have underlined **were.**
- Item 5: **My two grandmothers are friends.** You should have underlined **are.**
- Item 6: **I am late.** You should have underlined **am.**
6. Correct any mistakes.
7. Find part B on your worksheet. ✔
- Write sentences for each linking verb. Raise your hand when you've finished. (Observe students and give feedback.)
8. (Call on students to read their sentences.)

Answer Key: (Part B:) Answers will vary. Accept correct sentences.

Lesson 56

Materials: Each student will need a copy of the worksheet for lesson 56 (Blackline Master 56).

PRESENT-TENSE VERBS

Name _____

56

Lesson 56

- Verbs tell when the action in a sentence takes place.
- The name for the form of a verb that tells the time of the action is **tense.**
- **Present-tense** verbs express actions that happen now or that happen regularly. Present-tense verbs can also express things that are true most of the time.
- **Plural** subjects use the base form of present-tense verbs. Base forms of verbs don't have added endings.
- The subjects **I** and **you** also use the base form.
- **Singular** subjects usually add **s** or **es** to the base form.

Write the correct present-tense form of the verb to finish the sentence.

1. **jump**   She _____.
2. **run**   Frank and his dog _____.
3. **learn**   The students _____ quickly.
4. **like**   Ivan _____ pizza and ice cream.
5. **act**   Billy and I _____ in every play.
6. **seem**   You _____ to be unhappy today.
7. **teach**   Mr. Bauer _____ at Central High.
8. **win**   I hope Jason _____ the award.
9. **sound**   The alarms _____ every time we walk in the door.

BLM 56   201

1. Look at your worksheet for lesson 56. ✔
- Here's some more information about verbs. I'll read what it says. Follow along:

- Verbs tell when the action in a sentence takes place.
- The name for the form of a verb that tells the time of the action is **tense.**
- **Present-tense** verbs express actions that happen now or that happen regularly. Present-tense verbs can also express things that are true most of the time.
- **Plural** subjects use the **base form** of present-tense verbs. Base forms of verbs don't have added endings.
- The subjects **I** and **you** also use the base form.
- **Singular** subjects usually add **s** or **es** to the base form.

---

2. (Write on the board:)

---

1. **Ducks quack.**
2. **He falls.**
3. **I swim.**

- Example 1: **Ducks quack.** When is the action happening? (Ideas: *Now; always.*)
- Yes. That means the sentence takes a present-tense verb.
- What's the subject? (Signal.) *Ducks.*
- Is that singular or plural? (Signal.) *Plural.*
- So the sentence uses the base form of the verb: **quack.**
- Example 2: **He falls.** What's the subject? (Signal.) *He.*
- Is that singular or plural? (Signal.) *Singular.*
- So the sentence uses a base verb with **s** added: **falls.**
- Example 3: **I swim.**
- What's the subject? (Signal.) *I.*
- Is that singular or plural? (Signal.) *Singular.*
- What's the rule for the subjects **I** and **you**? (Idea: *Use the base form of the verb.*)
3. Complete your worksheet. Write the correct present-tense form of the verb to finish the sentence. Raise your hand when you've finished.
(Observe students and give feedback.)

4. (After the students complete the items, do a workcheck. For each item, call on a student to say whether the subject is singular or plural, say and spell the correct verb form, and read the complete sentence. If an answer is wrong, give the correct answer.)

Answer Key: 1. jumps **2.** run **3.** learn **4.** likes **5.** act **6.** seem **7.** teaches **8.** wins **9.** sound

Lesson 57

Materials: Each student will need a copy of the worksheet for lesson 57 (Blackline Master 57).

EXERCISE 1

PAST-TENSE VERBS

57

Lesson 57

Name _____

- **Past-tense** verbs express actions that have already happened.
- Past-tense verbs are usually formed by adding **d** or **ed** to the base verb.
- The form of past-tense verbs is the same for both singular and plural subjects.

A. Write the past-tense form of the verb to finish the sentence.

1. mow   Jamael _____ yards all last summer.
2. wait   Betsy _____ twenty minutes for Howard.
3. explore   The tourists _____ the mission ruins.
4. watch   I _____ in horror as the wall tumbled.
5. help   Kyle _____ his grandmother clean her attic.

B. For each item, circle the verb. Write present or past to show its tense.

                                        Tense

1. Gordon erased the first paragraph of his essay. _____
2. Do you object to the plan? _____
3. Jeanne boasted about her new computer. _____
4. Leslie talks too much! _____
5. Suzi smiles easily. _____

202 BLM 57

1. Look at your worksheet for lesson 57. ✔
- The box has some more information about verb tense. I'll read what it says. Follow along:

> - **Past-tense** verbs express actions that have already happened.
> - Past-tense verbs are usually formed by adding **d** or **ed** to the base verb.
> - The form of past-tense verbs is the same for both singular and plural subjects.

What's the name for verbs that express actions that have already happened? (Signal.) *Past tense.*
- How do you form past-tense verbs? (Idea: *By adding **d** or **ed** to the base verb.*)

2. Find part A on your worksheet. ✔
- For each item, you'll write the past-tense form of the verb to finish the sentence.
- For Item 1, the verb is **mow: Jamael _____ yards all last summer.** What's the past tense of **mow**? (Signal.) *Mowed.*
- Yes. You should finish the sentence by writing **mowed** on the blank.
3. Complete the items. Raise your hand when you've finished.
   (Observe students and give feedback.)
4. (After the students complete the items, do a workcheck. For each item, call on a student to say and spell the past-tense verb form and read the complete sentence. If an answer is wrong, give the correct answer.)

Answer Key: (Part A:) 1. mowed
2. waited **3.** explored **4.** watched **5.** helped

EXERCISE 2

PRESENT- AND PAST-TENSE VERBS

1. Find part B on your worksheet. ✔
- For each item, circle the verb. Write **present** or **past** to show its tense. Raise your hand when you've finished.
   (Observe students and give feedback.)
2. (After the students complete the items, do a workcheck. For each item, call on a student to say the verb, read the complete sentence, and identify the verb tense. If an answer is wrong, give the correct answer.)

Answer Key: (Part B:) 1. erased, past
2. object, present **3.** boasted, past **4.** talks, present **5.** smiles, present

EXERCISE 1

FUTURE-TENSE VERBS

Name _____

Lesson 58

- **Future-tense** verbs express actions that will happen in the future.
- The future tense is formed by using a **helping verb.**
- For most verbs, use the helping verb **will** to form the present tense.
- When the subject of a sentence is **I** or **we,** you can use the helping verb **shall** instead of **will.**

A. Write the future-tense form of the verb to finish the sentence. Remember to write the helping verb.

1. **perform**   I _____ my magic show next Sunday night.

2. **begin**   The show _____ at 8:00.

3. **close**   The theater doors _____ at 8:05.

4. **amaze**   The last trick I do _____ you!

B. For each item, circle the verb. Write **present, past,** or **future** to show its tense.

                                           Tense

1. We shall attend your graduation ceremony.   _____

2. I learned a lot in computer camp last summer.   _____

3. Dan interviewed three people for the job.   _____

4. Piper writes advertisements.   _____

5. Oscar will compose a song for our party.   _____

BLM 58   203

1. Look at your worksheet for lesson 58. ✔
- You're going to learn about another verb tense. Follow along as I read what's in the box:

- **Future-tense** verbs express actions that will happen in the future.
- The future tense is formed by using a **helping verb.**
- For most verbs, use the helping verb **will** to form the future tense.
- When the subject of a sentence is **I** or **we,** you can use the helping verb **shall** instead of **will.**

- What's the name for verbs that express actions that will happen in the future? (Signal.) *Future tense.*
- How do you form most future-tense verbs? (Idea: *By using the helping verb* **will** *before the base verb.*)
2. For each item, write the future-tense form of the verb to finish the sentence. Remember to write the helping verb.
- For Item 1, the verb is **perform:** **I _____ my magic show next Sunday.** The subject's **I,** so what's the future tense of **perform?** (Ideas: *Shall perform; will perform.*)
- Yes. Finish the sentence by writing **shall** or **will perform** on the blank.
3. Complete the rest of the items. Raise your hand when you've finished. (Observe students and give feedback.)
4. (After the students complete the items, do a workcheck. For each item, call on a student to say and spell the past-tense verb form and read the complete sentence. If an answer is wrong, give the correct answer.)

Answer Key: (Part A:) 1. shall perform **or** will perform **2.** will begin **3.** will close **4.** will amaze **or** shall amaze **5.** will attend **or** shall attend **6.** will interview **7.** will compose

EXERCISE 2
VERB TENSES

1. Find part B on your worksheet. ✔
- For each item, circle the verb. Write **present, past,** or **future** to show its tense. Raise your hand when you've finished.
  (Observe students and give feedback.)

2. (After the students complete the items, do a workcheck. For each item, call on a student to say the verb, read the complete sentence, and identify the verb tense. If an answer is wrong, give the correct answer.)

Answer Key: (Part B:) 1. (shall attend), future **2.** (learned), past **3.** (interviewed), past **4.** (writes), present **5.** (will compose), future

Materials: Each student will need a copy of the worksheet for lesson 59 (Blackline Master 59).

USING VERB TENSES CONSISTENTLY

59
Lesson 59

Name _____

If the verb tenses in a sentence aren't consistent, rewrite the sentence to make them consistent. If the tenses are consistent, don't rewrite the sentence.

1. Mustafa jumps up and stomped out of class.

_____

2. The band played loudly and marches badly.

_____

3. Mr. Drummond will speak to our group, then he will take questions.

_____

4. The boss summons Wayne to the office and yelled at him.

_____

5. Chelsea selected the colors and paints her house.

_____

204 *BLM 59*

---

1. Let's review what you've learned about verb tenses.
- What's the name for verbs that express actions that happen now? **(Signal.)** *Present tense.*
- What's the name for verbs that express actions that have already happened? **(Signal.)** *Past tense.*
- What's the name for verbs that express actions that will happen in the future? **(Signal.)** *Future tense.*
2. When you write a sentence, you should use verb tenses consistently. You shouldn't switch from one tense to another.

3. (Write on the board:)

> **He walked into the office and asks for Ms. Phillips.**

- Look at the Example: **He walked into the office and asks for Ms. Phillips.**
- What's the first verb in the sentence? **(Signal.)** *Walked.* What tense? **(Signal.)** *Past.*
- What's the second verb? **(Signal.)** *Asks.* What's its tense? **(Signal.)** *Present.*
- One verb is past tense and one is present tense. That's not consistent. Make both verbs past tense. What's the new sentence? **(Idea:** *He walked into the office and asked for Ms. Phillips.*)
4. Find your worksheet for lesson 59. ✔
- If the verb tenses in a sentence aren't consistent, rewrite the sentence to make them consistent. If the tenses are consistent, don't rewrite the sentence.
- Item 1: **Mustafa jumps up and stomped out of class.**
- What's the first verb in the sentence? **(Signal.)** *Jumps.* What tense? **(Signal.)** *Present.*
- What's the second verb? **(Signal.)** *Stomped.* What's the tense? **(Signal.)** *Past.*
- Make the tenses consistent. What's the new sentence? **(Ideas:** *Mustafa jumps up and stomps out of class. Mustafa jumped up and stomped out of class.*)

5. Do the rest of the items. Raise your hand when you've finished.
   (Observe students and give feedback.)
6. (Call on a student to read each rewritten sentence. If the verb tenses are inconsistent, help students correct them.)

Answer Key: (Ideas:)

1. Mustafa jumps up and stomps out of class. Mustafa jumped up and stomped out of class.

2. The band played loudly and marched badly.
   The band plays loudly and marches badly.
3. (correct)
4. The boss summons Wayne to the office and yells at him.
   The boss summoned Wayne to the office and yelled at him.
5. Chelsea selected the colors and painted her house.
   Chelsea selects the colors and paints her house.

Materials: Each student will need a copy of the worksheet for lesson 60 (Blackline Master 60).

USING VERB TENSES CONSISTENTLY

> **60**
>
> Name _____
> **Lesson 60**
>
> ¹Gabe stared down from his apartment window. ²He sees his friends, Rafe and Lucky, on the street below. ³Rafe wears a top hat. ⁴Lucky wore a red cape. ⁵Lucky tripped. ⁶He grabs a garbage can. ⁷Gabe laughed out loud. ⁸Rafe and Lucky look up at Gabe. ⁹Rafe smiled. ¹⁰He bows deeply to Gabe.
>
> Rewrite only the sentences in the passage that use present-tense verbs. Change the verbs to past tense.
>
> _____
> _____
> _____
> _____
> _____
> _____
> _____
> _____
> _____
> _____
> _____
> _____
> _____
>
> BLM 60   205

1. You've learned that when you write a sentence, you should use verb tenses consistently.
2. That's also true when you write a paragraph. Don't switch back and forth from one tense to another.
3. Look at your worksheet for lesson 60. ✔
- The paragraph describes something that happened in the past, but some of its sentences use present-tense verbs.
- I'll read the paragraph, one sentence at a time. After each sentence, tell me the verb. Then tell me its tense.
- **Gabe stared down from his apartment window.** What's the verb? (Signal.) *Stared.*
  What tense? (Signal.) *Past.*

- **He sees his friends, Rafe and Lucky, on the street below.** What's the verb? (Signal.) *Sees.*
  What tense? (Signal.) *Present.*
- **Rafe wears a top hat.** What's the verb? (Signal.) *Wears.*
  What tense? (Signal.) *Present.*
- **Lucky wore a red cape.** What's the verb? (Signal.) *Wore.*
  What tense? (Signal.) *Past.*
- **Lucky tripped.** What's the verb? (Signal.) *Tripped.*
  What tense? (Signal.) *Past.*
- **He grabs a garbage can.** What's the verb? (Signal.) *Grabs.*
  What tense? (Signal.) *Present.*
4. (Repeat for the rest of the sentences.)
5. Five of the sentences have verbs that express the present tense. What are the numbers of these sentences? (Idea: *Sentences 2, 3, 6, 8, and 10.*)
6. Rewrite these sentences. Change the verbs to past tense. Raise your hand when you've finished.
   (Observe students and give feedback.)
7. (Call on a student to read each rewritten sentence and identify the correct verb tense. If the answer is wrong, give the correct answer.)

Answer Key:
2. He saw his friends, Rafe and Lucky, on the street below.
3. Rafe wore a top hat.
6. He grabbed a garbage can.
8. Rafe and Lucky looked up at Gabe.
10. He bowed deeply to Gabe.

Lesson 61

Materials: Each student will need a copy of the worksheet for lesson 61 (Blackline Master 61).

EXERCISE 1
ADJECTIVES

61

Lesson 61

Name _____

- **Adjectives** are words that describe nouns or pronouns.
- **Adjectives** answer the questions **what kind?** **how many?** or **which one?**
- More than one adjective may be used to describe a noun or pronoun.

A. For each item, underline the adjective and circle the word the adjective describes. Remember, more than one adjective can be used to describe the same word.

1. We grow pink petunias.
2. Old wooden houses are being rebuilt.
3. Gary collects rare gold coins.
4. Holly found seventeen shiny pennies.
5. Gino drives fast Italian cars.
6. I don't like chocolate yogurt.
7. Debra won't work with silly or lazy people.

B. Write **N** above the nouns, **P** above the pronouns, **V** above the verbs, and **A** above the adjectives.

1. Our two families quarreled.
2. Forecasters predict many hot, dry autumns.
3. They arranged wonderful parties.
4. My hometown is beautiful Dayton, Ohio.

206 BLM 61

1. Look at your worksheet for lesson 61. ✔
- You're going to work with another part of speech: **adjectives.**
- The box contains some information about adjectives. Follow along as I read:

> - **Adjectives** are words that describe nouns or pronouns.
>
> - Adjectives answer the questions **what kind**? **how many**? or **which one**?
>
> - More than one adjective may be used to describe a noun or pronoun.

- What are adjectives? (Idea: *Words that describe nouns or pronouns.*)

2. Here's an example: **Ten bicycles raced.** What's the adjective? (Signal.) *Ten.*
- What does **Ten** describe? (Signal.) *Bicycles.*
- What question does **Ten** answer about bicycles? (Idea: *How many bicycles raced.*)
3. Here's another example: **Angie bought big red balloons.** What's the first adjective? (Signal.) *Big.*
- What's the second adjective? (Signal.) *Red.*
- What do *big* and *red* describe? (Signal.) *Balloons.*
- What question do *big* and *red* answer about *balloons*? (Idea: *What kind of balloons Angie bought.*)
4. Find part A on your worksheet. ✔
- You're going to underline the adjective and circle the word the adjective describes. Remember, more than one adjective can be used to describe the same word. Raise your hand when you've finished.
(Observe students and give feedback.)
5. (After the students complete the items, do a workcheck. For each item, call on a student to say each adjective, name the word it describes, and tell what question it answers. If an answer is wrong, give the correct answer.)

Answer Key: Part A:
1. pink (petunias) 2. Old, wooden (houses)
3. rare, gold (coins) 4. seventeen, shiny (pennies) 5. fast, Italian (cars) 6. chocolate (yogurt) 7. silly, lazy (people)

EXERCISE 2

PARTS OF SPEECH

1. Let's review the parts of speech you've learned so far.
- What part of speech names people, places, things, ideas, or feelings? (Signal.) *Nouns.*
- What are pronouns? (Idea: *Words that can replace nouns.*)
- What part of speech expresses action? (Signal.) *Verbs.*
- What are adjectives? (Idea: *Words that describe nouns or pronouns.*)
2. Find part B on your worksheet. ✔
- For each item, write **N** above the nouns, **P** above the pronouns, **V** above the verbs, and **A** above the adjectives. Raise your hand when you've finished. (Observe students and give feedback.)

3. (Write on the board:)

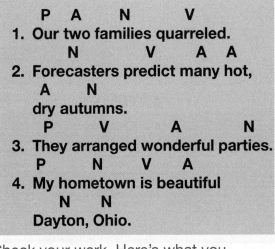

   P A N V
1. **Our two families quarreled.**
   N   V A A
2. **Forecasters predict many hot,**
  A N
  dry autumns.
   P   V   A   N
3. **They arranged wonderful parties.**
   P N   V A
4. **My hometown is beautiful**
     N   N
  Dayton, Ohio.

4. Check your work. Here's what you should have.

Lesson 62

Materials: Each student will need a copy of the worksheet for lesson 62 (Blackline Master 62).

ARTICLES

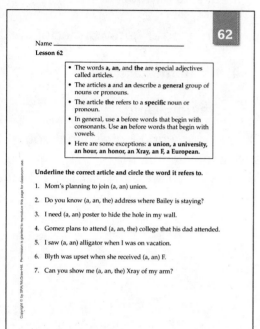

1. Look at your worksheet for lesson 62. ✔
- The box contains some information about a special kind of adjective. Follow along as I read:

> - The words **a, an,** and **the** are special adjectives called **articles.**
>
> - The articles **a** and **an** describe a **general** group of nouns or pronouns.
>
> - The article **the** refers to a **specific** noun or pronoun.
>
> - In general, use **a** before words that begin with consonants. Use **an** before words that begin with vowels.
>
> - Here are some exceptions: **a union, a university, an hour, an honor, an X ray, an F, a European.**

- What are the words **a, an,** and **the** called? (Signal.) *Articles.*
2. Here's an example of a sentence that has an article: **A peach can be sweet.** What's the article? (Signal.) *A.*
- What does **A** refer to? (Signal.) *Peach.*
- Yes, it refers to **any** peach.
- If you change **peach** to **apple,** what would the article be? (Signal.) *An.*
- That's right. **Peach** begins with a consonant, so the article is **a. Apple** begins with a vowel, so the article is **an.**
3. Here's another sentence: **The peach is sour.** What's the article? (Signal.) *The.*
- What does **The** refer to? (Signal.) *Peach.*
- Yes, one specific peach in a group.
4. For each item, you're going to underline the article and circle the word that it refers to.
   (Observe students and give feedback.)
- Item 1: **Mom's planning to join (a, an) union.**
- What's the article? (Signal.) *A.*
- Yes, **union** begins with a consonant sound, but it is one of the exceptions given in the box. Underline **a.**
5. Do the rest of the items. Raise your hand when you've finished.
6. (After the students complete the items, do a workcheck. For each item, call on a student to say each article and name the word it describes. If an answer is wrong, give the correct answer.)

Answer Key:
1. a (union) 2. the (address) 3. a (poster) 4. the (college) 5. an (alligator) 6. an F 7. the (X ray)

EXERCISE 1
DEMONSTRATIVE ADJECTIVES

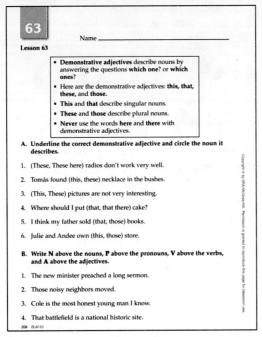

1. Look at your worksheet for lesson 63. ✔
- The box contains some more information about adjectives. Follow along as I read:

- **Demonstrative adjectives** describe nouns by answering the questions **which one?** or **which ones?**

- Here are the demonstrative adjectives: **this, that, these,** and **those.**

- **This** and **that** describe singular nouns.

- **These** and **those** describe plural nouns.

- **Never** use the words **here** and **there** with demonstrative adjectives.

- What's the name for the words **this, that, these,** and **those?** (Signal.) *Demonstrative adjectives.*
- What questions do demonstrative adjectives answer? (Idea: *Which one or which ones?*)
2. Here's an example of a sentence that has a demonstrative adjective: **This cap is too small.** What's the demonstrative adjective? (Signal.) *This.*
- What does **This** describe? (Signal.) *Cap.*
- What question does **This** answer about **cap?** (Idea: *Which one is too small?*)
- That's right. **This** is singular. It answers a question about one cap.
3. Here's another example: **These here tables need to be cleared.**
- What's wrong with the sentence? (Idea: *You shouldn't use **here** with **These.***)
- How do you make it correct? (Idea: *These tables need to be cleared.*)
- What does **These** describe? (Signal.) *Tables.*
- What question does **These** answer about **tables?** (Idea: *Which ones need to be cleared?*)
4. Find part A on your worksheet. ✔
- Underline the correct demonstrative adjective and circle the noun it describes. Raise your hand when you've finished.
  (Observe students and give feedback.)
5. (After the students complete the items, do a workcheck. For each item, call on a student to say each adjective and name the noun it describes. If an answer is wrong, give the correct answer.)

Answer Key: Part A:
1. These (radios) **2.** that (necklace) **3.** These (pictures) **4.** that (cake) **5.** those (books) **6.** this (store)

EXERCISE 2

PARTS OF SPEECH

1. Find part B on your worksheet. ✔
• For each item, write **N** above the nouns, **P** above the pronouns, **V** above the verbs, and **A** above the adjectives. Raise your hand when you've finished.
   (Observe students and give feedback.)

2. (Write on the board:)

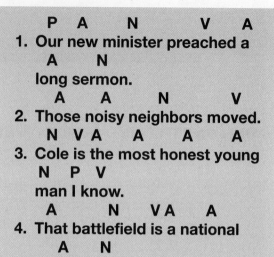

```
            P  A   N      V   A
1. Our new minister preached a
       A    N
   long sermon.
       A    A     N      V
2. Those noisy neighbors moved.
   N  V  A   A    A     A
3. Cole is the most honest young
   N  P  V
   man I know.
       A    N      V A    A
4. That battlefield is a national
           A    N
   historic site.
```

3. Check your work. Here's what you should have. Fix any mistakes.

COMPARATIVE AND SUPERLATIVE ADJECTIVES

> **64**
>
> Name _____
> Lesson 64
>
> - **Comparative** adjectives compare one noun or pronoun with another.
> - To form comparatives of most short adjectives, add the ending **er**.
> - To form comparatives of longer adjectives, use the word **more**.
> - **Superlative** adjectives compare one noun or pronoun with several others.
> - To form superlatives of most short adjectives, add the ending **est**.
> - To form superlatives of longer adjectives, use the word **most**.
>
> Write the comparatives and superlatives of each adjective.
>
> | | Comparative | Superlative |
> |---|---|---|
> | 1. famous | _____ | _____ |
> | 2. rich | _____ | _____ |
> | 3. delicious | _____ | _____ |
> | 4. slow | _____ | _____ |
>
> B. Write two sentences for each adjective. In the first sentence, use the comparative. In the second sentence, use the superlative.
>
> A. beautiful
>
> 1. _____
> 2. _____
>
> B. young
>
> 3. _____
> 4. _____
>
> BLM 64 209

1. Look at your worksheet for lesson 64. ✔
- Here's some more information about adjectives. Follow along as I read:

> - **Comparative** adjectives compare one noun or pronoun with another.
>
> - To form comparatives of most short adjectives, add ending **er.**
>
> - To form comparatives of longer adjectives, use the word **more.**
>
> - **Superlative** adjectives compare one noun or pronoun with several others.
>
> - To form superlatives of most short adjectives, add the ending **est.**
>
> - To form superlatives of longer adjectives, use the word **most.**

2. What's the name for adjectives that compare one noun or pronoun with another? (Signal.) *Comparatives.*
- So, to compare the sizes of England and Russia, you might say: **England is smaller than Russia.**
- What's the comparative adjective? (Signal.) *Smaller.*
- Yes, **small** is a short adjective. You add the ending **er** to make it comparative.
- To compare how successful Joel and Kurt are, you might say: **Joel is more successful than Kurt.**
- What's the comparative adjective? (Signal.) *More successful.*
- Right. **Successful** is a longer adjective, so you use the word **more** to make it comparative.
3. What's the name for adjectives that compare one noun or pronoun with several others? (Signal.) *Superlatives.*
- Listen. To compare how fast Toby was to how fast the other runners were, you might say: **Toby was the fastest runner.**
- What's the superlative adjective? (Signal.) *Fastest.*
- **Fast** is a short adjective, so you add the ending **est** to make it superlative.
- To compare how popular Labrador retrievers are to how popular other breeds of dogs are, you might say: **Labrador retrievers are the most popular of all breeds of dogs.**
- What's the superlative adjective? (Signal.) *Most popular.*
- Because **popular** is a longer adjective, you use the word **most** to make it superlative.

4. Find part A on your worksheet. ✔
• You're going to write the comparatives and superlatives of each adjective. Raise your hand when you've finished.
  (Observe students and give feedback.)
5. (Write on the board:)

> 1. **more famous, most famous**
> 2. **richer, richest**
> 3. **more delicious, most delicious**
> 4. **slower, slowest**

6. Here's what you should have. Correct any mistakes.

Answer Key: Part B:
Accept all reasonable answers.

IRREGULAR COMPARATIVE AND SUPERLATIVE ADJECTIVES

> **65**
> Lesson 65
> Name _____
>
> - Comparatives and superlatives of some adjectives are **irregular**. This means they're not formed by adding **er** or **est** or by using the words **more** or **most**.
> - Here are some common adjectives that have irregular comparatives and superlatives:
>
> | | | |
> |---|---|---|
> | bad . . . . .worse | / | worst |
> | good . . . . . . .better | / | best |
> | little . . . . .less | / | least |
>
> To finish the sentences, write comparatives and superlatives of the underlined adjective.
>
> **A. This year, our team is bad.**
>
> 1. It's _____ than last year's team.
>
> 2. It's the _____ team we've ever had.
>
> **B. Neil is a good student.**
>
> 3. He's a _____ student than Josh is.
>
> 4. He's probably the _____ student in our school.
>
> **C. This job requires little skill.**
>
> 5. It requires _____ skill than my other job.
>
> 6. In fact, it requires the _____ skill of any job I've ever had.
>
> 210 BLM 65

1. Let's review comparative and superlative adjectives.
- How do you form comparatives of most short adjectives? (Idea: *By adding* **er.**)
- How do you form comparatives of longer adjectives? (Idea: *By using* **more.**)
- How do you form superlatives of most short adjectives? (Idea: *By adding* **est.**)
- How do you form superlatives of longer adjectives? (Idea: *By using* **most.**)
2. Look at your worksheet for lesson 65. ✔
- Here's some more information about adjectives.

> - Comparatives and superlatives of some adjectives are **irregular.** This means they're not formed by adding **er** or **est** or by using the words **more** or **most.**

> - Here are some common adjectives that have irregular comparatives and superlatives:
>
> | | | |
> |---|---|---|
> | **bad** . . . . .worse | / | **worst** |
> | **good** . . . .better | / | **best** |
> | **little** . . . . .less | / | **least** |

3. You're going to write comparatives and superlatives of the underlined adjectives to finish the sentences.
- For Item 1, the adjective is **bad: This year, our team is bad.**
- Sentence 1: **It's _____ than last year's team.** What's being compared? (Idea: *This year's team to last year's team.*)
- That's two things. Do you say **It's badder than last year's team**? (Signal.) *No.*
- What's the comparative for **bad**? (Idea: *Worse.*) Write **worse** on the blank.
- Sentence 2: **It's the _____ team we've ever had.** What's being compared? (Idea: *This year's team to all past teams.*)
- That's more than two things, so do you say, **It's the baddest team we've ever had?** (Signal.) *No.*
- What's the superlative for **bad**? (Signal.) *Worst.* Write **worst.**
4. Do the rest of the items. Raise your hand when you've finished.
   (Observe students and give feedback.)
5. (After the students complete the items, do a workcheck. For each item, call on a student to read the sentences. If an answer is wrong, say the correct answer.)

Answer Key: 1. worse **2.** worst **3.** better **4.** best **5.** less **6.** least

Lesson 66

EXERCISE 1
ADVERBS

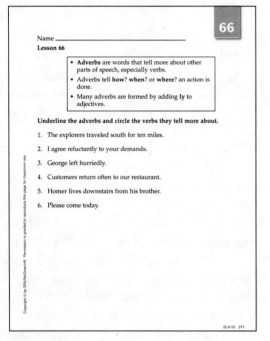

1. Look at your worksheet for lesson 66. ✔
- You're going to learn about another part of speech: **adverbs.**
- The box contains some information about adverbs. Follow along as I read:

> - **Adverbs** are words that tell more about other parts of speech, especially verbs.
>
> - Adverbs tell **how**? **when**? or **where**? an action is done.
>
> - Many adverbs are formed by adding **ly** to adjectives.

- If a word tells more about verbs, what part of speech is it? (Signal.) *An adverb.*

2. Here's an example: **The ballerina danced gracefully.** What's the adverb? (Signal.) *Gracefully.*
- Yes, **gracefully** tells more about the verb **danced.** What does it tell? (Idea: *How the ballerina danced.*)
3. Here's another example: **The storm moved north.** What's the adverb? (Signal.) *North.*
- What word does it tell more about? (Idea: *Moved.*)
- What part of speech is **moved**? (Idea: *A verb.*)
- What does **north** tell about? (Idea: *Where the storm moved.*)
4. Here's another example: **He arrived late.** What's the adverb? (Signal.) *Late.*
- What word does it tell more about? (Idea: *Arrived.*)
- What does **late** tell about? (Idea: *When he arrived.*)
- Do **north** and **late** end in **ly?** (Signal.) *No.*
- No, but they're still adverbs. Remember, not all adverbs end in **ly.**
5. You're going to underline the adverbs and circle the verbs they tell more about. (Observe students and give feedback.)
6. (After the students complete the items, do a workcheck. For each item, call on a student to say the adverb and the verb it tells more about. If an answer is wrong, say the correct answer.)

Answer Key: Part A: 1. south (traveled)
2. reluctantly (agree) **3.** hurriedly (left) **4.** often (return) **5.** downstairs (lives) **6.** today (come)

> **Materials:** Each student will need a copy of the worksheet for lesson 67 (Blackline Master 67).

USING ADVERBS AND ADJECTIVES CORRECTLY

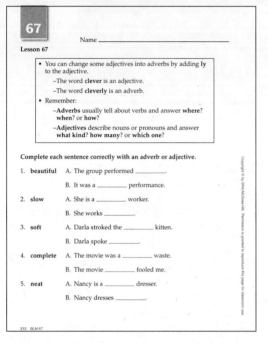

1. Look at your worksheet for lesson 67. ✔
- Here's some information about adverbs and adjectives. Follow along:

- You can change some adjectives into adverbs by adding **ly** to the adjective.

  –The word **clever** is an adjective.

  –The word **cleverly** is an adverb.

- Remember:

  –**Adverbs** usually tell about verbs and answer **where**? **when**? or **how**?

  –**Adjectives** describe nouns or pronouns and answer **what kind**? **how many**? or **which one**?

---

2. Each item has an adjective and a pair of incomplete sentences. You'll use the adjective to complete one of the sentences. For the other sentence, you'll change the adjective to an adverb by adding the letters **ly**.

3. Item 1: The adjective is **beautiful.**
- Sentence A is **The group performed _____.** To finish the sentence you need a word that tells about the verb **performed,** and tells more about *how* the group performed. So the correct word for the sentence is **beautifully.** Sentence A is: **The group performed beautifully.**
- Sentence B is **It was a _____ performance.** To finish this sentence, you need a word that tells more about the noun **performance.** So the correct word for the sentence is **beautiful.** Sentence B is **It was a beautiful performance.**

4. Look at item 2. The adjective is **slow.** What's the adverb? (Signal.) *Slowly.*
- Write the word that completes sentence A. Then write the word that completes sentence B.

  (Observe students and give feedback.)
- Check your work. For item 2, sentence A should be **She is a slow worker.** Sentence B should be **She works slowly.**

5. Do the rest of the items. Raise your hand when you've finished.

  (Observe students and give feedback.)

6. Check your work.
- Item 3: Sentence A should be **Darla stroked the soft kitten.** Sentence B should be **Darla spoke softly.**

- Item 4: Sentence A should be **The movie was a complete waste.** Sentence B should be **The movie completely fooled me.**
- Item 5: Sentence A should be **Nancy is a neat dresser.** Sentence B should be **Nancy dresses neatly.**

7. Raise your hand if all your answers are correct. Otherwise, fix any mistakes.

Lesson 68

Materials: Each student will need a copy of the worksheet for lesson 68 (Blackline Master 68).

PREPOSITIONS

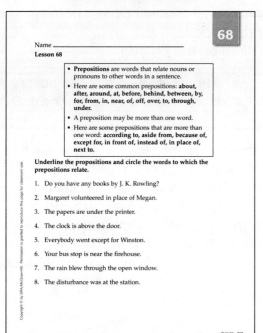

1. Look at your worksheet for lesson 68. ✔
- You're going to learn about another part of speech: **prepositions.**
- Here's some information about prepositions. Follow along:

- **Prepositions** are words that relate nouns or pronouns to other words in a sentence.

- Here are some common prepositions: **about, after, around, at, before, behind, between, by, for, from, in, near, of, off, over, through.**

- A preposition may be more than one word.

- Here are some prepositions that are more than one word: **according to, aside from, because of, except for, in front of, instead of, in place of, next to.**

- What are prepositions? (Idea: *Words that relate nouns or pronouns to other words in a sentence.*)
2. Here's an example sentence: **The trail beside the river is lovely.** The preposition is **beside.** It relates **trail** and **river.**
3. Here's another example sentence: **Tyler is standing in front of Wendy.** What's the preposition? (Idea: *In front of.*)
- **In front of** is a preposition that has more than one word. What two things are related by **in front of** ? (Idea: *Tyler and Wendy.*)
4. For each item, underline the prepositions and circle the words that the prepositions relate.
- Item 1: **Do you have any books by J. K. Rowling**? What's the preposition? (Signal.) *By.*
- What words are related? (Idea: *Books, J. K. Rowling.*)
5. Do the rest of the items. Raise your hand when you've finished.
(Observe students and give feedback.)

Answer Key: Part A:
1. by (books, J. K. Rowling) **2.** in place of (Margaret, Megan) **3.** under (papers, printer)
4. above (clock, door) **5.** except for (Everyone, Winston) **6.** near (bus stop, firehouse) **7.** through (rain, window)
8. at (disturbance, station)

Lesson 69

Materials: Each student will need a copy of the worksheet for lesson 69 (Blackline Master 69).

PREPOSITIONAL PHRASES

1. What are prepositions? (Idea: *Words that relate nouns or pronouns to other words in a sentence.*)
2. Look at your worksheet for lesson 69. ✔
• Here's some more information about prepositions. Follow along:

> • A **prepositional phrase** is a group of words that begins with a preposition and ends with a noun or pronoun.
>
> • The noun or pronoun at the end of a prepositional phrase is called the **object of the preposition.**

• What's the name for a group of words that begins with a preposition and ends with a noun or pronoun? (Signal.) *Prepositional phrase.*

• What's the name for that noun or pronoun? (Signal.) *Object of the preposition.*
3. (Write on the board:)

> 1. **The club meets in the library.**
> 2. **Barb lives around the corner.**

• Sentence 1: **The club meets in the library.** The prepositional phrase is **in the library.** It begins with the preposition **in** and ends with the noun **library.**
• Sentence 2: **Barb lives around the corner.** What's the prepositional phrase? (Idea: *Around the corner.*)
• What's the preposition? (Signal.) *Around.*
• What's the object of the preposition? (Signal.) *Corner.*
4. You're going to write the prepositional phrase. In the phrase that you write, underline the preposition and circle the object of the preposition.
• Item 1: **The driver of the car stopped suddenly.** What's the prepositional phrase? (Idea: *Of the car.*) Write the phrase.
• What's the preposition? (Signal.) *Of.*
• So you underline **of.** What's the object of the preposition? (Signal.) *Car.*
• Circle **car.**
5. Do the rest of the items. Raise your hand when you've finished.
(Observe students and give feedback.)
6. (After the students complete the items, do a workcheck. For each item, call on a student to say the prepositional phrase, the preposition, and the object of the preposition. If an answer is wrong, say the correct answer.)

Answer Key: Part A:
1. <u>of</u> the (car) **2.** <u>behind</u> her (house) **3.** <u>on</u> the (fence) **4.** <u>after</u> the (show)

PARTS OF SPEECH

1. Find part B on your worksheet. ✔
- Write **N** above nouns, **P** above pronouns, **V** above verbs, **A** above adjectives, **AD** above adverbs, and **PR** above prepositions. Raise your hand when you've finished.

(Observe students and give feedback.)

2. (Write on the board:)

```
        N    V    AD   PR   A
1. Sam walked slowly into the
        N
   museum.
     N  V  A  A   A   N   PR
2. Ivy put the rusty trash can near
     A   A   N
   the back door.
     A   N  V    V
3. The rally was cancelled
              PR  N
   because of rain.
```

3. Check your work. Here's what you should have.

Lesson 70

Materials: Each student will need a copy of the worksheet for lesson 70 (Blackline Master 70).

CONJUNCTIONS

1. Look at your worksheet for lesson 70. ✔
- Let's talk about another part of speech: **conjunctions.**
- The box contains some information about conjunctions. Follow along:

- **Conjunctions** are words that connect parts of a sentence.

- Here are some common conjunctions: **and, but, nor, or.**

- Sometimes conjunctions are more than one word: **either . . . or, neither . . . nor, both . . . and, not only . . . but also.**

- What parts of speech are these words: **and, but, nor,** and **either . . . or?** (Signal.) *Conjunctions.*

2. Here's an example sentence: **Send your e-mails and faxes to my new address.** What's the conjunction? (Signal.) *And.*
- What parts of the sentence are joined by **and**? (Idea: *e-mails and faxes.*)
3. Here's another example: **Jenny will go either to tennis camp or swimming camp this summer.** What's the conjunction? (Signal.) *Either . . . or.*
- What parts of the sentence are joined by **either . . . or**? (Idea: *tennis camp, swimming camp.*)
4. Here's another example: **Rita shopped but bought nothing.** What's the conjunction? (Signal.) *But.*
- What parts of the sentence are joined by **but**? (Idea: *Shopped, bought nothing.*)
5. It's your turn. Underline the conjunctions and circle the two parts of the sentence they join. Remember, some conjunctions are more than one word.
- Item 1: **Chris watches but doesn't play rugby.** What's the conjunction? (Signal.) *But.*
- Underline **but.** What parts of the sentence does it join? (Idea: *Watches, doesn't play.*)
6. Do the rest of the items. Raise your hand when you've finished.
   (Observe students and give feedback.)

Answer Key: 1. but (watches, doesn't play) **2.** and (Karen, her father) **3.** or (potato chips, pretzels) **4.** Neither . . . nor (senator, congressman) **5.** Either . . . or (Ms. Bolton, Ms. Hernandez) **6.** or (get involved, do nothing) **7.** not only . . . but also (students, teachers)

Lesson 71

PARTS OF SPEECH

71

Lesson 71

Name —————————

Write **N** above nouns, **P** above pronouns, **V** above verbs, **A** above
adjectives, **AD** above adverbs, **PR** above prepositions, and **C** above
conjunctions.

1. Grant and Anne sang five funny songs.

2. Albert slept peacefully under the old oak tree.

3. You won, but I played a better game.

4. Golden eagles often fly and hunt near our lodge.

5. Is Elise a poet or a painter?

6. Neither Mexico nor Korea sent a representative to the meeting in
Sweden.

7. These new shoes hurt my feet badly.

216 BLM 71

1. Let's review the parts of speech you've learned.
- What part of speech names people, places, things, ideas, or feelings? (Signal.) *Nouns.*
- What are pronouns? (Idea: *Words that can replace nouns.*)
- What part of speech expresses action? (Signal.) *Verbs.*
- What part of speech describes nouns and pronouns? (Signal.) *Adjectives.*
- What part of speech tells where, when, or how an action is done? (Signal.) *Adverbs.*
- What part of speech relates nouns or pronouns to other words in a sentence? (Signal.) *Prepositions.*

2. Look at your worksheet for lesson 71. ✔

- Write **N** above nouns, **P** above pronouns, **V** above verbs, **A** above adjectives, **AD** above adverbs, **PR** above prepositions, and **C** above conjunctions. Raise your hand when you've finished.
(Observe students and give feedback.)

3. (Write on the board:)

```
      N    C   N    V    A    A
1. Grant and Anne sang five funny
      N
   songs.
      N    V        AD      PR   A
2. Albert slept peacefully under the
   A   A   N
   old oak tree.
      P    V   C   P   V   A   A
3. You won, but I played a better
      N
   game.
      A      N      AD  V  C  V
4. Golden eagles often fly and hunt
   PR   P   N
   near our lodge.
      V   N   A   N   C   A   N
5. Is Elise a poet or a painter?
      C       N       C     N   V   A
6. Neither Mexico nor Korea sent a
            N       PR  A   N   PR
   representative to the meeting in
      N
   Sweden.
      A    A    N    V   P   N
7. These new shoes hurt my feet
   AD
   badly.
```

4. Check your work. Here's what you should have.

Lesson 72

SUBJECT–VERB AGREEMENT

Name _____
Lesson 72

- The main word in a subject is a **noun** or **pronoun**.
- The main word in a predicate is a **verb**.
- The main word in the subject must **agree in number** with the main verb in the predicate. This means:
  —If the main noun or pronoun is **singular**, the verb has to be **singular**.
  —If the main noun or pronoun is **plural**, the verb has to be **plural**.

Circle the main word in the subject. Write **S** on the blank if the subject is singular, **P** if it is plural. Underline the verb that agrees in number with the subject.

1. _____ Space travel (interests, interest) me.
2. _____ Betty and Sara (shares, share) a birthday.
3. _____ (Does, Do) tangerines grow on trees?
4. _____ This snake's fangs (contains, contain) some poison.
5. _____ The birds' nest (sits, sit) on the tree branch.
6. _____ Lilacs only (blooms, bloom) in the early spring.

BLM 72 217

1. Let's review what you know about subjects and predicates.
- The **subject** is the part of the sentence that tells whom or what the sentence is about.
- The **predicate** is the part of the sentence that tells what the subject is, does, or is like.
2. Look at your worksheet for lesson 72. ✔
- Here's some more information about subjects and predicates. Follow along:

- The main word in a subject is a **noun** or **pronoun**.
- The main word in a predicate is a **verb**.
- The main word in the subject must **agree in number** with the main verb in the predicate. This means:

  —If the main noun or pronoun is **singular,** the verb is **singular.**

  —If the main noun or pronoun is **plural,** the verb is **plural.**

3. (Write on the board:)

> 1. **Lou's latest idea deserves our consideration.**
> 2. **Jay's silly jokes makes me laugh out loud.**

- Sentence 1: **Lou's latest idea deserves our consideration.**
- The complete subject is **Lou's latest idea.** The main noun is **idea.** That's because it's the idea, not Lou, that deserves our consideration.
- The complete predicate is **deserves our consideration.** The main verb is **deserves.**
- **Idea** is singular, so the main verb is singular, too.
- In this sentence, the subject and verb agree in number.
- Sentence 2: **Jay's silly jokes makes me laugh out loud.** What's the full subject? (Idea: *Jay's silly jokes.*)
- What's the main word in the subject? (Idea: *Jokes.*)

- Is **jokes** singular or plural? (Signal.) *Plural.*
- What's the complete predicate? (Idea: *Makes me laugh out loud.*)
- What's the main verb? (Idea: *Makes.*)
- Is **makes** singular or plural? (Signal.) *Singular.*
- So, do the subject and verb agree in number? (Signal.) *No.*
- What should the main verb be? (Idea: *Make.*)

4. You're going to circle the main word in the subject. Write **S** on the blank if the subject is singular and **P** if it is plural. Then underline the verb that agrees in number with the subject.
(Observe students and give feedback.)

5. (After the students complete the items, do a workcheck. For each item, call on a student to say the main word in the subject, tell whether it is singular or plural, and say the verb that agrees with the subject. If an answer is wrong, give the correct answer.)

Answer Key:
1. S, (travel) interests 2. P, (Betty and Sara) share 3. P, (tangerines) Do 4. P, (fangs) contain 5. S, (nest) sits 6. P, (lilacs) bloom

Lesson 73
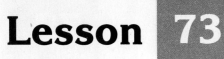

Materials: Each student will need a copy of the worksheet for lesson 73 (Blackline Master 73).

COMPOUND SUBJECTS

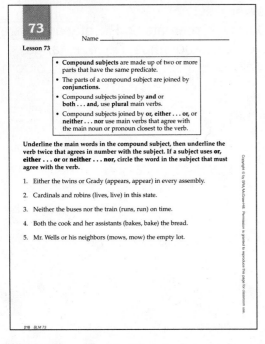

1. Remember, the **subject** of a sentence is the part that tells whom or what the sentence is about. The **predicate** is tells what the subject is, does, or is like.
2. Look at your worksheet for lesson 73. ✔
• The box contains additional information about subjects. Follow along as I read:

> • **Compound subjects** are made up of two or more parts that have the same predicate.
>
> • The parts of a compound subject are joined by **conjunctions**.
>
> • Compound subjects joined by **and** or **both . . . and,** use **plural** main verbs.

> • Compound subjects joined by **or, either . . . or,** or **neither . . . nor** use main verbs that agree with the main noun or pronoun closest to the verb.

• What's the name for a subject that has two or more parts? (Signal.) *Compound subject.*
• What part of speech joins the parts of a compound subject? (Signal.) *Conjunctions.*
3. (Write on the board:)

> **Kitty and Emily know the lock combination.**

• Look at the example: **Kitty and Emily know the lock combination. Kitty and Emily** are the main words in the compound subject. The subject is plural, so the sentence uses a plural verb, **know.**
4. Underline the main words in the compound subject, then underline the verb twice that agrees in number with the subject. If a subject uses **or, either . . . or** or **neither . . . nor,** circle the word in the subject that must agree with the verb.
5. Do the items. Raise your hand when you've finished.
(Observe students and give feedback.)
6. (After the students complete the items, do a workcheck. If an answer is wrong, give the correct answer.)

Answer Key:
1. twins, (Grady;) appears **2.** cardinals, (robins;) live **3.** buses, (train;) runs **4.** cook, (assistants;) bake **5.** Mr. Wells, (neighbors;) mow

Materials: Each student will need a copy of the worksheet for lesson 74 (Blackline Master 74).

COMPOUND PREDICATES

> Name _____
> **Lesson 74**
>
> 74
>
> • Compound predicates are made up of two or more parts that have the same subject.
> • The main words in compound predicates are verbs.
> • The parts of a compound predicate are joined by conjunctions.
> • Compound predicates always agree in number with the subject.
>
> **Circle the main word in the subject and underline the verbs that agree in number with the subject.**
>
> 1. My mother (sings, sing) and (dances, dance).
> 2. Tracey (sweeps, sweep) or (mops, mop) her floors every day.
> 3. Postal workers (sorts, sort) and (delivers, deliver) thousands of letters each day.
> 4. Martin either (hikes, hike) or (bikes, bike) in the fall.
> 5. Sally (reads, read) and (studies, study) novels.
>
> Copyright © by SRA/McGraw-Hill. Permission is granted to reproduce this page for classroom use.
>
> BLM 74 219

1. Let's review.
• What's the **subject** of a sentence? **(Idea:** *The part that tells whom or what the sentence is about.*)
• What are **compound subjects**? **(Idea:** *Subjects that are made up of two or more parts with the same predicate.*)
• What is the **predicate** of a sentence? **(Idea:** *The part that tells what the subject is, does, or is like.*)
• Now you're going to learn about **compound predicates.**
2. Look at your worksheet for lesson 74. ✔
• Follow along as I read:

> • **Compound predicates** are made up of two or more parts that have the same subject.

> • The main words in compound predicates are **verbs.**
> • The parts of a compound predicate are joined by **conjunctions.**
> • Compound predicates always **agree in number** with the subject.

• What are compound predicates? **(Idea:** *Predicates with two or more parts that have the same subject.*)
3. (Write on the board:)

> **Chuck both shoots and rebounds equally well.**

• Look at the example: **Chuck both shoots and rebounds equally well.** The subject is **Chuck.** That's singular. The compound predicate is **shoots and rebounds.** Each verb is also singular, so the subject and predicate agree in number.
4. It's your turn. Circle the main word in the subject and underline the verbs that agree in number with the subject.
5. Do the items. Raise your hand when you've finished.
   (Observe students and give feedback.)
6. (After the students complete the items, do a workcheck. If an answer is wrong, give the correct answer.)

Answer Key:
1. (mother;) sings, dances 2. (Tracey;) sweeps, mops 3. (workers;) sort, deliver 4. (Martin;) hikes, bikes 5. (Sally;) reads, studies

Lesson 75

Materials: Each student will need a copy of the worksheet for lesson 75 (Blackline Master 75).

COMMAS

```
  75        Name _____
Lesson 75

  • If a sentence contains a series of three or more items that are
    joined by a conjunction, commas are used to separate the items so
    that the meaning of the sentence is clear.
  • If a sentence contains only two items, it doesn't use a comma.
  • When separating a series of more than two items, place a comma
    before the conjunction.
  • The items separated by commas may either be words or groups of
    words, such as prepositional phrases.

Rewrite each sentence that needs commas to separate items. If a sentence
doesn't need commas, write correct.

  1.  Glenda is beautiful rich and famous.
      _____

  2.  I told you to water the plants check the mail and turn off the lights.
      _____

  3.  Does Greene's sell CD players DVD players or TV sets?
      _____

  4.  Mary sat in the shade and under an umbrella.
      _____

  5.  The trail leads over the hill near the woods and into the town.
      _____

  6.  Please notify David and Rocky about the time change.
      _____

220  BLM 75
```

1. **Commas** are punctuation marks used in writing to show readers where to pause in a sentence.
2. Look at your worksheet for lesson 75. ✔
- Here is a rule about commas. Follow along as I read:

> - If a sentence contains **a series of three or more items** that are joined by a conjunction, commas are used to separate the items so that the meaning of the sentence is clear.
>
> - If a sentence contains only two items, it **doesn't** use a comma.

> - When separating a series of more than two items, **place a comma before the conjunction.**
>
> - The items separated by commas may be either **words** or **groups of words,** such as prepositional phrases.

- Here's a sentence with a series of words that are separated by commas: **Foley stopped, looked, and listened before crossing the railroad tracks.**
- Here's a sentence with a series of phrases that are separated by commas: **Look for the kitten beneath the porch, in the shed, and behind the barn.**
3. Rewrite each sentence that needs commas to separate items. If a sentence doesn't need commas, write **correct.** (Observe students and give feedback.)
4. (After the students complete the items, do a workcheck. If the answer is wrong, say the correct answer.)

Answer Key:
1. Glenda is beautiful, rich, and famous.
2. I told you to water the plants, check the mail, and turn off the lights.
3. Ms. Greene sells CD players, DVD players, and TV sets.
4. (correct)
5. The trail leads over the hill, through the woods, and into the town.
6. (correct)

COMMAS IN INTRODUCTORY WORDS AND DIRECT ADDRESS

> 76
>
> Name _____
> Lesson 76
>
> - When a sentence begins with certain introductory words, such as **yes**, **no**, or **well**, use a comma to separate the word from the rest of the sentence.
> - When a sentence **addresses someone directly by name**, use a comma or commas to separate the name from the rest of the sentence.
> - If a sentence is just about someone, **don't** use commas to separate the name from the sentence.
>
> Rewrite the sentences and put commas where they belong. Some sentences may need more than one comma. If a sentence doesn't need commas, write **correct**.
>
> 1. Mr. Morris I believe the answer in the book is wrong.
>
> 2. Mr. Morris checked the answer in the book.
>
> 3. Well I can't understand why this phone doesn't work.
>
> 4. No you can't swim in the lake Michael.
>
> 5. Linda left most of her work undone.
>
> 6. Matt is angry Cathy because you hurt his feelings.
>
> BLM 76 221

1. Find your worksheet for lesson 76. ✔
- You're going to learn some more rules about commas. Here's one rule.

> - When a sentence begins with certain introductory words, such as **yes, no,** or **well,** use a comma to separate the word from the rest of the sentence.

- (Write on the board:)

> **1. Yes, I agree with you.**

- Look at example sentence 1: **Yes, I agree with you.** The comma separates the beginning word from the rest of the sentence.

2. Here are some other rules. Follow along:

> - When a sentence **addresses someone directly by name,** use a comma or commas to separate the name from the rest of the sentence.
> - If a sentence is just about someone, **don't** use commas to separate the name from the sentence.

- (Write on the board:)

> **2. Colin, I hear that you want to join the marines.**
> **3. I hear, Colin, that you want to join the marines.**
> **4. I hear that you want to join the marines, Colin.**
> **5. I hear that Colin wants to join the marines.**

- Sentence 2: **Colin, I hear that you want to join the marines.** This sentence addresses Colin directly. His name is at the beginning of the sentence, so the sentence has one comma after the name.
- Sentence 3: **I hear, Colin, that you want to join the marines.** This sentence also addresses Colin directly. This time, his name is in the middle of the sentence, so it has a comma before and a comma after the name.
- Sentence 4: **I hear that you want to join the marines, Colin.** This is another sentence that addresses Colin directly. This time his name is at the end of the sentence, so it has one comma before his name.

- Sentence 5: **I hear that Colin wants to join the marines.** This sentence is just about Colin. His name isn't separated from the sentence with commas.

3. You're going to rewrite the sentences and put commas where they belong. Some sentences may need more than one comma. If a sentence doesn't need commas, write **correct.**

4. Raise your hand when you've finished.

5. (After the students complete the items, do a workcheck. For each item, call on a student to read the sentence, indicating where commas are needed. If the answer is wrong, say the correct answer.)

Answer Key:

1. Mr. Morris, I believe the answer in the book is wrong.
2. (correct)
3. Well, I can't understand why this phone doesn't work.
4. No, you can't swim in the lake, Michael.
5. (correct)
6. Matt is angry, Cathy, because you hurt his feelings.

COMMAS IN DATES, PLACE NAMES, AND ADDRESSES

> **77**
> Lesson 77   Name _____
>
> - If a date has a month, day, and year, use a comma to separate the numbers of the day from the year.
> - Don't use a comma if the date has only the month and year.
> - Use a comma to separate the names of cities and the names of states or countries.
> - In an address, if the city name is used after a street name, use a comma to separate the street from the city.
> - In an address, don't use a comma after the state name if it is followed by a ZIP code.
>
> **Rewrite the sentences with dates or addresses that need commas or that use commas incorrectly. Some sentences may need more than one comma. If the date or address in a sentence is correct, write correct.**
>
> 1. I met Julie on January 6, 2001.
> _____
>
> 2. You can write to me at 24 Park Lane Benton Kentucky 42025.
> _____
>
> 3. The *Titanic* sank in April, 1912.
> _____
>
> 4. That company has its headquarters in Casper Wyoming.
> _____
>
> 5. The plane was headed for London England.
> _____
>
> 222   BLM 77

1. Look at your worksheet for lesson 77. ✔
- Here are some rules for using commas. Follow along:

> - If a date has a **month, day,** and **year,** use a comma to separate the numbers of the day from the year.
> - **Don't** use a comma if the date has only the **month** and **year.**

- (Write on the board:)

> 1. **March 191999**
> 2. **March 19, 1999**
> 3. **March 1999**

- Example 1: **March 191999.** You can't tell which numbers refer to the day of the month and which numbers refer to the year. The date needs a comma between the day and the year.
- Example 2: **March 19, 1999.** This is how to write the date.
- Example 3 shows how to write a date that doesn't have a day: **March 1999.**
2. Here are some more rules:

> - Use a comma to separate the **names of cities** and the **names of states or countries.**
> - In an **address,** if the city name is used after a street name, use a comma to separate the street from the city.
> - In an **address, don't** use a comma after the state name if it is followed by a ZIP code.

- (Write on the board:)

> 1. **Milwaukee, Wisconsin**
> 2. **905 Cove Street, Franklin, Tennessee**
> 3. **Waterbury, Connecticut 06705.**

- Example 1: **Milwaukee, Wisconsin.** You need a comma between the city name and the state name.
- Example 2: **905 Cove Street, Franklin, Tennessee.**
- This address has a comma between the street name and the city name. It has another comma between the city name and the state name.

77

- Example 3: **Waterbury, Connecticut 06705.** This address has a city name and a state name followed by a ZIP code. You **do** need a comma between the city name and the state name. You **don't** need a comma between the state and the ZIP code.

3. Rewrite the sentences with dates or addresses that need commas or that use commas incorrectly. Some sentences may need more than one comma. If the date or address in a sentence is correct, write **correct.**

   (Observe students and give feedback.)

4. (After the students complete the items, do a workcheck. For each item, call on a student to read the item, indicating where commas are needed. If the answer is wrong, say the correct answer.)

Answer Key:
1. (correct)
2. You can write to me at 24 Park Lane, Benton, Kentucky 42025.
3. The *Titanic* sank in April 1912.
4. That company has its headquarters in Casper, Wyoming.
5. The plane was headed for London, England.

Materials: Each student will need a copy of the worksheet for lesson 78 (Blackline Master 78).

COMMAS

Name _____
Lesson 78

78

Rewrite the sentences that need commas. Add commas where they're needed. Some sentences may need more than one comma. If a sentence doesn't need commas, write **correct.**

1. The streets were full of bicycles taxis trucks and buses.

2. Morgan has moved to 3907 Sunnydale Avenue, Austin, Texas 78712.

3. No that's absolutely not true Charlie.

4. The map led us around the barn down the path and over the fence.

5. My favorite state capital is Richmond Virginia.

6. Tony's great-grandfather came to the United States in June 1901.

7. Well what should we do now?

8. I'm sure Rosalind that the memorial is in Atlanta Georgia.

BLM 78   223

1. Let's review.
- What's the rule for using commas in a sentence that has a series of more than two items? (Idea: *Separate the items with commas.*)
- When a sentence begins with certain introductory words, such as **yes, no,** or **well,** what's the rule? (Idea: *Use a comma to separate the words from the rest of the sentence.*)
- What's the rule when a sentence **addresses someone directly** by name? (Idea: *Use a comma or commas to separate the name from the rest of the sentence.*)
- What if a sentence is just about someone, but isn't addressing that person directly? (Idea: *Don't use commas to separate the name from the sentence.*)

- What's the rule for using commas in place names? (Idea: *Put a comma between the name of the city and the name of the state.*)
- What's the rule for using commas in addresses? (Idea: *Put a comma between the name of the street and the name of the city, and put a comma between the name of the city and the name of the state.*)
- What if an address has a ZIP code? (Idea: *Don't put a comma between the name of the state and the ZIP code.*)

2. Look at your worksheet for lesson 78. ✔
- You're going to rewrite the sentences that need commas. Some sentences may need more than one comma. If a sentence doesn't need commas, write **correct.**

3. (After the students complete the items, do a workcheck. For each item, call on a student to read the sentence, indicating where commas are needed. If the answer is wrong, say the correct answer.)

Answer Key:
1. The streets were full of bicycles, taxis, trucks, and buses.
2. (correct)
3. No, that's absolutely not true, Charlie.
4. The map led us around the barn, down the path, and over the fence.
5. My favorite state capital is Richmond, Virginia.
6. (correct)
7. Well, what should we do now?
8. I'm sure, Rosalind, that the memorial is in Atlanta, Georgia.

Lesson 79

Materials: Each student will need a copy of the worksheet for lesson 79 (Blackline Master 79).

COMBINING SENTENCES

79

Lesson 79

Name _____

Rewrite each pair of sentences as a combined sentence.

1. The TV series is a police drama. It is realistic.

   _____

2. Wolfgang is rambunctious. He is a puppy.

   _____

3. Alonzo and Jerrod are volunteers. They are cheerful.

   _____

4. Denise is a golfer. She is a professional.

   _____

5. Dr. Higgins is a teacher. He is strict.

   _____

224 BLM 79

---

1. When two short sentences share information about a subject, you can sometimes combine them into one longer sentence. **Combining sentences** can make your writing sound better.

2. (Write on the board:)

   > **Melinda is friendly. She is a student.**

   - Here are two short sentences: **Marissa is friendly. She is a student.**

- What's the subject of the first sentence? **(Signal.)** *Marissa.*
- What's the subject of the second sentence? **(Signal.)** *She.*
- **She** is a pronoun. What do pronouns do? **(Idea:** *Replace nouns.***)**
- So in the second sentence, **She** replaces **Marissa.** Both sentences share information about Marissa: She is friendly and she is a student.
- Here's a combined sentence for this example: **Marissa is a friendly student.**

3. Look at your worksheet for lesson 79. ✔
- Rewrite each pair of sentences as a combined sentence.
- Number 1: **The TV series is a police drama. It is realistic.**
- Write a combined sentence for Number 1. Raise your hand when you've done that.
- Read your combined sentence. **(Idea:** *The TV series is a realistic police drama.***)** Write that sentence.

4. Write combined sentences for the rest of the items. Raise your hand when you've finished.

   (Observe students and give feedback.)

Answer Key: Ideas: Accept correct sentences.

COMBINING SENTENCES WITH CONJUNCTIONS

Name _____

Lesson 80

Use the conjunctions to rewrite each pair of sentences as a combined sentence.

1. **and** The morning was cold. It was rainy.

   _____

2. **or** Ernie may visit Alabama. He may visit Mississippi.

   _____

3. **but** The ride was short. It was fun.

   _____

4. **or** The Burts may buy a car. They may buy a SUV.

   _____

5. **and** Liz wore a blue sweater. She wore a plaid skirt.

   _____

6. **but** Steve is shy. He is nice.

   _____

BLM 80 225

1. What part of speech are these words: **and, but, or**? (Signal.) *Conjunctions.*

- Another way to make your writing more interesting is to combine information that is in two short sentences into one longer sentence. You use conjunctions to join the information that is about the same subject.

2. Look at your worksheet for lesson 80. ✔
- Use a conjunction to rewrite each pair of sentences as a combined sentence.
- Number 1: **The morning was cold. It was rainy.**
- What's the subject of the first sentence? (Signal.) *Morning.*
- What's the subject of the second sentence? (Signal.) *It.*
- So in the second sentence, **It** replaces **Morning.**
- Here's a combined sentence for Number 1. It uses the conjunction **and**: **The morning was cold and rainy.** Write that sentence.
- Number 2: **Ernie may visit Alabama. He may visit Mississippi.** Use the conjunction **or** to write a combined sentence. Raise your hand when you're finished.
- Read your combined sentence. (Idea: *Ernie may visit Alabama or Mississippi.*)

3. Use the conjunctions to write combined sentences for the rest of the items. Raise your hand when you've finished. **(Observe students and give feedback.)**

Answer Key: Ideas: Accept correct sentences.

Lesson 81

Materials: Each student will need a copy of the worksheet for lesson 81 (Blackline Master 81).

COMPOUND SENTENCES

> **81**
>
> Lesson 81
>
> Name _____
>
> - **Compound sentences** are two complete sentences that are linked with the conjunctions **and, but,** or **or.**
> - In a compound sentence, **use a comma** before the conjunction.
>
> Rewrite the pairs of sentences as compound sentences. Use the conjunctions. Remember to put commas where they're needed.
>
> 1. **and** Amy opened the window. Dust blew into her room.
>
> 2. **or** We'll talk to the principal. We'll go to the school board meeting.
>
> 3. **and** Katrina began to play. The crowd became silent
>
> 4. **but** Ricky had tickets. He couldn't get into the stadium.
>
> 5. **or** Libby can leave now. She can wait for us.
>
> 6. **but** Grandpop is old. He is very fast.
>
> 226 BLM 81

1. Another way to make your writing more interesting is to use **compound sentences.**
2. Look at your worksheet for lesson 81. ✔
- Here's some information about compound sentences. Follow along as I read:

> - **Compound sentences** are two complete sentences that are linked with the conjunctions **and, but,** or **or.**
>
> - In a compound sentence, **use a comma** before the conjunction.

- What's the name for two complete sentences that are linked with conjunctions? (Signal.) *Compound sentences.*

3. (Write on the board:)

> 1. **I stopped by your house. You weren't home.**
> 2. **I sopped by your house, but you weren't home.**

- Look at Example 1: **I stopped by your house. You weren't home.** Each sentence is complete. Each one has a subject and predicate.
- Example 2 is a compound sentence: **I stopped by your house, but you weren't home.** The sentence combines the two short sentences with the conjunction **but** and a **comma.**
4. You're going to rewrite the pairs of sentences as compound sentences. Use the conjunctions. Remember to put commas where they're needed.
- Find Number 1: **Amy opened the window. Dust blew into her room.** Use the conjunction **and** and a comma to write a combined sentences. Raise your hand when you've done that.
- Read your combined sentence. Indicate where the comma is needed. (Idea: *Amy opened the window, and dust blew into her room.*)
- Make sure that you put the comma before the conjunction, and that you didn't use a capital letter to begin **dust.**
5. It's your turn. Do the rest of the items. Raise your hand when you've finished. (Observe students and give feedback.)

Answer Key: Ideas: Accept correct sentences.

COMPOUND SENTENCES

> **82**
>
> Name _____
> Lesson 82
>
> **A.** If an item is a compound sentence, write **compound**. If it isn't a compound sentence, write **no**.
>
> 1. _____ Is the tent in the front yard or in the garage?
> 2. _____ I want to have a party, but I can't invite everyone.
> 3. _____ Eli wants to play hockey, and he wants to be a goalie.
> 4. _____ The storm was powerful but brief.
> 5. _____ The horse was breathing hard and sweating.
>
> **B.** Use the conjunctions to rewrite each pair of sentences as a compound sentence. Put commas where they're needed.
>
> 1. **or** Buck said he would clean his room. He would study.
> _____
> 2. **but** The plane left on time. It arrived an hour late.
> _____
> 3. **and** Valerie was embarrassed. She wanted to hide her face.
> _____
> 4. **but** Stu found the safe. He didn't know the combination.
> _____
>
> BLM 82 227

1. What's a compound sentence? (Idea: *Two complete sentences that are linked with a conjunction.*)
2. Find your worksheet for lesson 82. ✔
- All these sentences contain one of the conjunctions **and, but,** or **or.**
- Some of the sentences are compound sentences and some aren't. If an item is a compound sentence, write **compound.** If it isn't a compound sentence, write **no.**

- Item 1: **Is the tent in the front yard or in the garage**?
- **Is the tent in the front yard**? Is that a complete sentence? (Signal.) *Yes.*
- **In the garage.** Is that a complete sentence? (Signal.) *No.* Write **no** for Item 1.
3. Do the rest of the items. Raise your hand when you've finished.
   (Observe students and give feedback.)
4. (After the students complete the items, do a workcheck. For each item, call on a student to read the item and tell if it is a compound sentence. If the answer is wrong, say the correct answer.)

Answer Key: Part A: 1. no **2.** compound **3.** compound **4.** no **5.** no

Part B:
1. Buck said he would clean his room, or he would study.
2. The plane left on time, but it arrived an hour late.
3. Valerie was embarrassed, and she wanted to hide her face.
4. Stu found the safe, but he didn't know the combination.

Lesson 83

EXERCISE 1
CONTRACTIONS

83
Lesson 83

Name _____

- **Contractions** are words that are made by combining two words and leaving out one or more letters.
- Use **apostrophes** in contractions to show where letters have been left out.

Common Contractions

aren't	/	are not	isn't	/	is not
doesn't	/	does not	she'll	/	she will
didn't	/	did not	she's	/	she has, she is
hasn't	/	has not	they'll	/	they will
here's	/	here is	they've	/	they have
he'll	/	he will	we'll	/	we will
he's	/	he has, he is	we're	/	we are
I'm	/	I am	you'll	/	you will

A. Write the two words that make each contraction.

1. _____ You'll need to bring lunch.
2. _____ Congress hasn't passed that bill.
3. _____ My dog didn't obey the command.
4. _____ Barney isn't sure that he can go with us.
5. _____ Look, here's the map we need.

B. For each item, underline the two words that can make a contraction. Write the contractions on the blanks.

1. _____ I am going to Hillary's birthday party!
2. _____ She has invited ten people.
3. _____ She will give us ice cream and cake.
4. _____ After we eat, we will play games.
5. _____ Her brother says he is going to do magic tricks.

228 BLM 83

1. Look at your worksheet for lesson 83. ✔
- The box contains some information about **contractions.** I'll read it. Follow along:

> - **Contractions** are words that are made by combining two words and leaving out one or more letters.
>
> - Use **apostrophes** in contractions to show where letters have been left out.

- The list below the box shows some common contractions and the words that make them.
2. Find part A. ✔
- Write the two words that make each contraction.

- Item 1: **You'll need to bring lunch.** What's the contraction? (Signal.) *You'll.*
- What two words make **You'll**? (Signal.) *You will.* Write those words on the blank.
3. Do the rest of the items. Raise your hand when you've finished.
(Observe students and give feedback.)
4. Now find part B on your worksheet. ✔
- Underline two words that can make contractions. Write the contractions on the blanks.
- Look at the first sentence: **I am going to Hillary's birthday party!**
- What two words can make a contraction? (Signal.) *I am.*
- What's the contraction for **I am**? (Signal.) *I'm.*
- That's right (spell): **I[apostrophe]m** is the contraction for **I am.**
5. Do the rest of the items. Raise your hand when you've finished.
(Observe students and give feedback.)
6. (After the students complete A and B, do a workcheck. For each item in part A, call on a student to say the two words that make a contraction. For each item in part B, call on a student to say the two words that make the contraction. Then have them say and spell the contraction. Have students say "apostrophe" to show where apostrophes are needed. If the answer is wrong, say the correct answer.)

Answer Key: Part A: 1. you will **2.** has not
3. did not **4.** is not **5.** here is
Part B: 1. I am, I'm **2.** She has, She's
3. She will, She'll **4.** We will, we'll **5.** he is, he's

Materials: Each student will need a copy of the worksheet for lesson 84 (Blackline Master 84).

CONTRACTIONS AND HOMOPHONES

Name _____
Lesson 84

Homophones	Contractions
1. there, their	they're
2. theirs	there's
3. your	you're
4. its	it's

If a sentence is correct, write **correct**. If a sentence uses a homophone instead of the correct contraction, rewrite it so that it uses two words that make the correct contraction.

[1]Kirsten and her family are moving. [2]Their buying an old Victorian house. [3]Its the biggest house on the block. [4]Your not going to believe how many rooms it has. [5]It has four floors. [6]Theirs a kitchen on each floor. [7]Kirsten says there planning to turn the house into a bed-and-breakfast.

1. _____
2. _____
3. _____
4. _____
5. _____
6. _____
7. _____

BLM 84   229

1. Some contractions can be confused with other words that sound the same but are spelled differently and have different meanings.
* The name for words like this is **homophones.**
2. Look at your worksheet for lesson 84. ✔
* Here are some words that sound like contractions but aren't:

homophones	
1. there, their	they're
2. theirs	there's
3. your	you're
4. its	it's

* Look at Item 1. The word **there** is about location: **There is the building.** The other word **their** is a possessive pronoun for **they: Their building is over there.** The word **they're** is a contraction for **they are: They're in the building.** Remember, contractions *always* have apostrophes.
* Look at item 2. Do you know what part of speech the word **theirs** is? (Idea: *A possessive pronoun*)
* Yes, **theirs** shows that **they** own or have something: **The building is theirs.**
* The word **there's** is a contraction for **there is: There's the building.** How do you know it's a contraction? (Idea: *It has an apostrophe.*)
* Example 3. **Your** is another possessive pronoun. It shows that **you** own or have something: **I like your new bike.**
* The word **you're** is a contraction for **you are: You're early for class.**
* Item 4. What part of speech is **its**? (Idea: *A possessive pronoun.*)
* (Spell) **I-t-s** shows that **it** owns something. Does the possessive have an apostrophe? (Signal.) *No.*
* No, (spell) **i-t-apostrophe-s** is a contraction for **it is: It's about time you got here.**
3. The paragraph has numbered sentences. If a sentence is correct, write **correct**. If a sentence uses a homophone instead of a contraction, rewrite it so that it uses two words that make the correct contraction. Raise you're hand when you're finished.

(Observe students and give feedback.)

4. (After the students complete the items, do a workcheck. For each item, call on a student to say the wrong word and tell the two words that make the correct contraction. If the answer is wrong, say the correct answer.)

Answer Key:
1. (correct)
2. They are buying an old Victorian house.
3. It is the biggest house on the block.
4. You are not going to believe how many rooms it has.
5. (correct)
6. There is a kitchen on each floor.
7. Kirsten says they are planning to turn the house into a bed-and-breakfast.

Materials: Each student will need a copy of the worksheet for lesson 85 (Blackline Master 85).

ANTONYMS

85

Name _____

Lesson 85

Fill in the circle next to the word that is an **antonym** for the underlined word.

1. Colby's long journey across the mountains left him feeling <u>weary</u>.
   ○ tired   ○ worried   ○ rested

2. If we're going to win the election, we must <u>unite</u> our supporters.
   ○ divide   ○ organize   ○ educate

3. The evil prince was especially <u>cruel</u> to the poor.
   ○ mean   ○ kind   ○ royal

4. Be <u>cautious</u> when you use these chemicals, or they'll explode.
   ○ careful   ○ careless   ○ thoughtful

5. I can never understand Mr. Kelly's <u>complicated</u> instructions.
   ○ simple   ○ difficult   ○ loud

6. This poem is by an <u>obscure</u> poet that few people know about.
   ○ unknown   ○ famous   ○ bad

7. Ari took a <u>temporary</u> job until he could find a job he really wants.
   ○ boring   ○ short   ○ permanent

8. That silly duck hat makes you look <u>ridiculous</u>.
   ○ funny   ○ large   ○ sensible

9. Brian is so <u>arrogant</u> he thinks he's the only person who knows anything.
   ○ humble   ○ rude   ○ lonely

230 *BLM 85*

1. **Antonyms** are words that have opposite meanings.
- Writers sometimes use antonyms to make their writing more interesting.
2. What's the name for words that have opposite meanings? (Signal.) *Antonyms.*
- An antonym for **hot** is **cold.** An antonym for **up** is **down.**
- What's an antonym for **weak**? (Ideas: *Strong; powerful; mighty.*)
- What's an antonym for **easy**? (Ideas: *Hard; difficult; tough.*)
3. Look at your worksheet for lesson 85. ✔

- For each item, fill in the circle next to the word that is an antonym for the underlined word.
- Item 1: **Colby's long journey across the mountains left him feeling weary.** Look at the possible answers. From the sentence, you can figure out that Colby had a long, hard journey. So what does **weary** probably mean? (Idea: *Tired.*)
- Does **tired** mean the opposite of **weary**? (Signal.) *No.*
- No, it means the same thing. Does **worried** mean the opposite of **weary**? (Signal.) *No.*
- No, **worried** doesn't fit the sentence. So what's left? (Signal.) *Rested.*
- That's right, the opposite of **weary** is **rested.** Fill in the circle next to that word.
4. Do the rest of the items. Read each sentence carefully to make sure you understand the meaning of the underlined word. Raise your hand when you've finished.
5. (After the students complete the items, do a workcheck. For each item, call on a student to say the antonym for the underlined word. If the answer is wrong, say the correct answer.)

Answer Key: 1. rested **2.** divide **3.** kind **4.** careless **5.** simple **6.** famous **7.** permanent **8.** sensible **9.** humble

Lesson 86

Materials: Each student will need a copy of the worksheet for lesson 86 (Blackline Master 86).

SYNONYMS

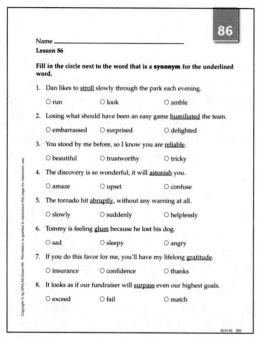

1. What are **antonyms**? (Idea: *Words that mean the opposite of each other.*)
2. Now you're going to work with words that mean almost the same thing. They're called **synonyms.**
   - Writers sometimes use synonyms, as well as antonyms, to make their writing more interesting.
   - A synonym for **fix** is **repair.** A synonym for **begin** is **start.**
   - What's a synonym for **stop**? (Ideas: *Halt; quit; end.*)
   - What's a synonym for **small**? (Ideas: *Tiny; little.*)
3. Look at your worksheet for lesson 86. ✔

- For each item, you're going to fill in the circle next to the word that is a synonym for the underlined word.
- Item 1: **Dan likes to stroll slowly through the park each evening.** Look at the possible answers. From the sentence, you can tell that Dan likes to go through the park. So what does **stroll** mean? (Idea: *Walk.*)
- Walk how? (Signal.) *Slowly.*
- Does **run** mean the same thing as **walk slowly**? (Signal.) *No.*
- No, it means the opposite. Does **look** mean the same thing as **walk slowly**? (Signal.) *No.*
- No, **look** doesn't fit the sentence. So what's left? (Signal.) *Amble.*
- That's right, **amble** means almost the same thing as **stroll.** Fill in the circle next to that word.
4. Do the rest of the items. Read each sentence carefully to make sure you understand the meaning of the underlined word. Raise your hand when you've finished.
5. (After the students complete the items, do a workcheck. For each item, call on a student to say the synonym for the underlined word. If the answer is wrong, say the correct answer.)

Answer Key: 1. amble **2.** embarrassed **3.** trustworthy **4.** amaze **5.** suddenly **6.** sad **7.** thanks **8.** exceed

Materials: Each student will need a copy of the worksheet for lesson 87 (Blackline Master 87); the teacher and each student will need a copy of the same children's dictionary.

ANTONYMS AND SYNONYMS

87

Name _____

Lesson 87

A. Use the information in each passage to figure out the meaning of the underlined word. Fill in the circle next to the **antonym** for the underlined word. Use your dictionary to help.

1. The sisters are very different. Jenna is shy, and Rebecca is <u>extroverted</u>.

   ○ outgoing ○ tall ○ timid

2. The editor wanted to <u>delete</u> the story from the paper. The publisher wanted it to stay in.

   ○ keep ○ remove ○ copy

3. The first speech was <u>tedious</u>. The second one, however, was lively.

   ○ interesting ○ dull ○ short

B. Fill in the circle next to the **synonym** for the underlined word. Use your dictionary to help.

1. The sisters are very different. Jenna is shy, and Rebecca is <u>extroverted</u>.

   ○ outgoing ○ tall ○ timid

2. The editor wanted to <u>delete</u> the story from the paper. The publisher wanted it to stay in.

   ○ keep ○ remove ○ copy

3. The first speech was <u>tedious</u>. The second one, however, was lively.

   ○ interesting ○ dull ○ short

232 BLM 87

Copyright © by SRA/McGraw-Hill. Permission is granted to reproduce this page for classroom use.

1. Let's review.
- What are **antonyms**? (Idea: *Words that mean the opposite of each other.*)
- What are **synonyms**? (Idea: *Words that mean almost the same thing.*)
2. Look at part A on your worksheet for lesson 87. ✔
- Use the information in each passage to figure out the meaning of the underlined word. Fill in the circle next to the **antonym** for the underlined word. Use your dictionary for help.

- Item 1: **The sisters are very different. Jenna is shy, and Rebecca is extroverted.**
- What word does the sentence tell you is the antonym or opposite of **shy**? (Signal.) *Extroverted.*
- So what does **extroverted** mean? (Ideas: *Not shy; outgoing.*)
- So fill in the circle next to **outgoing**.
3. Do the rest of the items in part A. Raise your hand when you've finished. (Observe students and give feedback.)
4. Now find part B on your worksheet. ✔
- Here are the same passages that you read in part A. This time, you'll fill in the circle next to the **synonym** for the underlined word. Use your dictionary for help. Raise your hand when you've finished. (Observe students and give feedback.)
5. (After the students complete part A and B, do a workcheck. For each item, call on a student to say the antonym or synonym for the underlined word. If the answer is wrong, say the correct answer.)

Answer Key: Part A: 1. timid **2.** keep **3.** interesting
Part B: 1. outgoing **2.** remove **3.** dull

Lesson 88

Materials: Each student will need a copy of the worksheet for lesson 88 (Blackline Master 88); the teacher and each student will need a copy of the same children's dictionary.

USING CONTEXT CLUES

Name _____

Lesson 88

88

Answer the questions about the paragraphs. Use your dictionary.

Paragraph 1

The senator gave her usual **monotonous** speech about spending too much. We'd heard the speech so often, it almost to put us to sleep. I wish she'd find something more interested to talk about.

Questions

1. What part of speech is <u>monotonous</u>? _____

2. What clues in the context help you figure out what <u>monotonous</u> means?
_____

3. What does <u>monotonous</u> probably mean?
_____

Paragraph 2

When Harriet is sad, Andrew can always **cajole** her into feeling better. He tells Harriet how pretty she looks, how smart she is, and how much people like being around her.

Questions

1. What part of speech is <u>cajole</u>? _____

2. What clues in the context help you figure out what <u>cajole</u> means?
_____

3. What does <u>cajole</u> probably mean?
_____

BLM 88   233

1. The sentence or paragraph in which a word appears is called the **context.**
- Sometimes you can figure out the meaning of a word you don't know by looking at its context. For example, the context may also have an antonym or a synonym that helps you figure out the word's meaning.
- Context can give other clues to word meanings besides antonyms and synonyms.
2. Look at your worksheet for lesson 88. ✔
- Follow along as I read the first paragraph:

> The senator gave her usual **monotonous** speech. We'd heard the speech so often, it almost put us to sleep. I wish she'd find something more interesting to talk about.

3. Find the three questions for the paragraph.
- Question 1 is: **What part of speech is monotonous?** What's the answer? (Signal.) *Adjective.*
- Yes, **monotonous** tells what kind of speech. Write **adjective** for Question 1.
- Question 2: **What clues in the context help you figure out what monotonous** means? (Ideas: *Almost put us to sleep; find something more interested to talk about.*) Write your answer for question 2.
- Question 3: **What does monotonous probably mean?** Use the information from the context to figure it out. (Ideas: *Dull; boring; uninteresting.*) Write your answer to Question 3.
- Now check your answer. Look up **monotonous** in your dictionary. Raise your hand when you've found it.
- What's the dictionary definition for **monotonous**? (Idea: *Boring, dull, uninteresting, routine.*)
- Yes, the senator's speech was boring or dull. If the answer you wrote is wrong, correct it.
- Follow along as I read the second paragraph:

> When Harriet is sad, Andrew can always **cajole** her into feeling better. He tells Harriet how pretty she looks, how smart she is, and how much people like being around her.

4. Find the three questions for the paragraph. ✔
- Question 1 is: **What part of speech is cajole?** What's the answer? (Signal.) *Verb.*

- Yes, **cajole** tells what Andrew does. Write **verb** for Question 1.
- Question 2: **What clues in the context help you figure out what** <u>cajole</u> **means?** (Ideas: *He tells Harriet how pretty she looks, how smart she is, and how much people like being around her.*) Write your answer for Question 2.
- Question 3: **What does** <u>cajole</u> **probably mean?** Use the information from the context to figure it out. (Ideas: *Flatter; coax; charm; sweet talk.*) Write your answer to Question 3.

- Now check your answer. Look up **cajole** in your dictionary. Raise your hand when you've found it.
- What's the dictionary definition for **cajole**? (Ideas: *Coax; flatter.*)
- Yes, Andrew can coax or flatter Harriet into feeling better. If the answer you wrote is wrong, correct it.

Lesson 89

Materials: Each student will need a copy of the worksheet for lesson 89 (Blackline Master 89); the teacher and each student will need a copy of the same children's dictionary.

USING CONTEXT CLUES

89

Lesson 89

Name _____

A. Answer the questions about the paragraph. Use your dictionary.

Paragraph

The king's **impertinence** was unbearable to his people. He insulted them. He called them names. Finally, they told him they would no longer put up with his ill-mannered behavior.

Questions

1. What part of speech is <u>impertinence</u>? _____

2. What clues in the context help you figure out what <u>impertinence</u> means?
   _____

3. What does <u>impertinence</u> probably mean?
   _____

B. Rewrite each sentence. Replace the underlined words with **monotonous, cajole,** or **impertinence.**

1. Your <u>rudeness</u> hurts my feelings.
   _____

2. That radio station plays <u>boring</u> music.
   _____

3. Amos tried to <u>coax</u> Martha to enter the beauty contest.
   _____

234 BLM 89

---

1. Look at part A on your worksheet for lesson 89. ✔
- Follow along as I read the paragraph:

> The king's **impertinence** was unbearable to his people. He insulted them. He called them names. Finally, they told him they would no longer put up with his ill-mannered behavior.

2. Find the three questions for the paragraph. ✔
- Question 1 is: **What part of speech is impertinence?** (Signal.) *Noun.* Write **noun** for Question 1.

- Question 2: **What clues in the context help you figure out what impertinence means?** (Ideas: *Insulted; ill-mannered.*) Write your answer for Question 2.
- Question 3: **What does impertinence probably mean?** Use the information from the context to figure it out. (Ideas: *Rudeness; disrespect.*) Write your answer to Question 3.
- Now check your answer. Look up **impertinence** in your dictionary. If the answer you wrote is wrong, correct it.
3. Find part B on your worksheet. ✔
- You've learned the words **monotonous, cajole,** and **impertinence.** Rewrite the sentences. Use one of the words to replace each underlined words. Raise your hand when you've finished. (Observe students and give feedback.)
4. (After the students complete the items, do a workcheck. For each item, call on a student to read the rewritten sentence. If the answer is wrong, say the correct answer.)

Answer Key: Part B:
1. Your <u>impertinence</u> hurts my feelings.
2. That radio station plays <u>monotonous</u> music.
3. Amos tried to <u>cajole</u> Martha to enter the beauty contest.

Lesson 90

Materials: Each student will need a copy of the worksheet for lesson 90 (Blackline Master 90); the teacher and each student will need a copy of the same children's dictionary.

USING CONTEXT CLUES

Name _____

Lesson 90

A. Answer the questions about the paragraph. Use your dictionary.

Paragraph

The agents entered the country **covertly**. No one saw them, and no one knew who they were. They were able to sneak into the city without being seen.

Questions

1. What part of speech is <u>covertly</u>? _____

2. What clues in the context help you figure out what <u>covertly</u> means?

3. What does <u>covertly</u> probably mean?

B. Rewrite each sentence. Replace the underlined words with monotonous, cajole, impertinence, or covertly.

1. The shoplifter <u>secretly</u> slipped the CD under his jacket.

2. The waiter's <u>rudeness</u> made us leave the restaurant.

3. Don't tell us that <u>boring</u> story again!

4. Can I <u>coax</u> you into lending me your calculator?

BLM 90 235

1. Look at part A on your worksheet for lesson 90. ✔
- Follow along as I read the paragraph:

> The agents entered the country **covertly.** No one saw them, and no one knew who they were. They were able to sneak into the city without being seen.

2. Find the three questions for the paragraph.
- Question 1 is: **What part of speech is covertly?** What's the answer? (Signal.) *Adverb.* Write **adverb** for Question 1.

- Question 2: **What clues in the context help you figure out what covertly means?** (Ideas: *No one saw them, and no one knew who they were. They were able to sneak into the city without being seen.*) Write your answer for Question 2.
- Question 3: **What does covertly probably mean?** Use the information from the context to figure it out. (Idea: *Secretly.*) Write your answer to Question 3.
- Check your answer. Look up **covertly** in your dictionary. If the answer you wrote is wrong, correct it.
3. Now find part B on your worksheet. ✔
- You've learned the words **monotonous, cajole, impertinence,** and **covertly.** Rewrite the sentences. Use one of the words to replace each underlined words. Raise your hand when you've finished. (Observe students and give feedback.)
4. (After the students complete the items, do a workcheck. For each item, call on a student to read the rewritten sentence. If the answer is wrong, say the correct answer.)

Answer Key: Part B:
1. The shoplifter <u>covertly</u> slipped the CD under his jacket.
2. The waiter's <u>impertinence</u> made us leave the restaurant.
3. Don't tell us that <u>monotonous</u> story again!
4. Can I <u>cajole</u> you into lending me your calculator?

Lesson 91

Materials: Each student will need a copy of the worksheet for lesson 91 (Blackline Master 91); the teacher and each student will need a copy of the same children's dictionary.

SIMILES

91

Lesson 91

Name _____

- **Similes** are expressions used in speech and writing to compare things that aren't really alike.
- Similes always use the words **like** or **as**.

Answer the questions about each simile. Use your dictionary.

Reba's smile is like the sun.

1. What two things are compared? _____

2. How are they similar? _____

Beau is as strong as a bull.

3. What two things are similar? _____

4. How are they similar? _____

My cousin walks like a duck.

5. What two things are similar? _____

6. How are they similar? _____

236   BLM 91

1. **Figures of speech** are expressions that speakers and writers use when they want us to picture something clearly in our minds.

2. Find your worksheet for lesson 91. ✔

- The box contains some information about one kind of figure of speech: **similes.** Follow along as I read:

> - **Similes** are expressions used in speech and writing to compare things that aren't really alike.
>
> - Similes always use the words **like** or **as.**

- What's the name of one kind of expression that compares things that aren't really alike? (Signal.) *Similes.*

- What words are always used in similes? (Signal.) ***Like* or *as.***

3. Here's an example of a simile: **The leaves covered Jonas like a blanket.**

- What two things are compared? (Idea: *Leaves and a blanket.*)

- How can leaves be like a blanket? (Ideas: *They both can cover Jonas; they both can keep him warm.*)

- So we can imagine this picture: leaves covering Jonas the way a blanket would.

4. Here's another simile: **This cake is as hard as a rock.**

- What two things are compared? (Idea: *Cake and rock.*)

- How can a cake be the same as a rock? (Ideas: *They're both difficult to cut; both could hurt your teeth if you bit into them.*)

- The simile helps us picture a cake that's so hard it can't be eaten.

5. You're going to answer the questions about three similes. Use your dictionary for help. Raise your hand when you've finished.
   (Observe students and give feedback.)

6. (After the students complete the items, do a workcheck. For each item, call on a student to answer the questions. If the answer is wrong, say the correct answer.)

Answer Key: 1. Reba's smile and the sun.
2. Ideas: Both are very bright; both shine; both are warm. **3.** Beau and a bull.
4. Ideas: Both are powerful; both are big.
5. My cousin and a duck. **6. Idea:** Both waddle.

Materials: Each student will need a copy of the worksheet for lesson 92 (Blackline Master 92); the teacher and each student will need a copy of the same children's dictionary.

SIMILES

Name _____

Lesson 92

Answer the questions about each simile. Use your dictionary.

It's like midnight in this room!

1. What two things are compared? _____

2. How are they similar? _____

Chandra's laugh is as sweet as honey.

3. What two things are compared? _____

4. How are they similar? _____

Deena is a timid as a mouse.

5. What two things are compared? _____

6. How are they similar? _____

BLM 92   237

---

1. Let's review.
- What are **figures of speech**? (Idea: *Expressions that speakers and writers use when they want us to picture something clearly in our minds.*)
- What's the name for figures of speech that use the words **like** or **as** to compare things that are not really alike? (Signal.) *Similes.*

2. Here's a simile: **Her hair is like silk.**
- What two things are compared? (Idea: *Hair and silk.*)
- How can hair be like silk? (Ideas: *Both are smooth; both are soft.*)
3. Here's another simile: **The baby is as precious to us as gold.**
- What two things are compared? (Idea: *The baby and gold.*)
- How is a baby the same as gold? (Ideas: *They're both very valuable; both are treasures.*)
4. Look at your worksheet for lesson 92. ✔
5. You're going to answer the questions about three similes. Use your dictionary to help you answer the questions. Raise your hand when you've finished. (Observe students and give feedback.)
6. (After the students complete the items, do a workcheck. For each item, call on a student to answer the questions. If the answer is wrong, say the correct answer.)

Answer Key: 1. midnight and a room **2. Idea:** Both are very dark. **3.** Chandra's laugh and honey **4. Ideas:** Both are pleasant; both are sugary. **5.** Deena and a mouse **6. Ideas:** Both are quiet; both are shy.

Lesson 93

Materials: Each student will need a copy of the worksheet for lesson 93 (Blackline Master 93); the teacher and each student will need a copy of the same children's dictionary.

METAPHORS

93

Name _____

Lesson 93

- **Metaphors** are another kind of expression used in speech and writing to compare things that aren't really alike.
- Metaphors **don't** use the words **like** or **as.**

Answer the questions about each metaphor. Use your dictionary.

The tornado was an angry child.

1. What two things are compared? _____

2. How are they similar? _____

Marley is an encyclopedia.

3. What two things are compared? _____

4. How are they similar? _____

Our classroom is a freezer.

5. What two things are compared? _____

6. How are they similar? _____

238 BLM 93

1. Find your worksheet for lesson 93. ✔
- Let's talk about another kind of figure of speech: **metaphors.**
- Follow along as I read what's in the box:

- **Metaphors** are another kind of expression used in speech and writing to compare things that aren't really alike.

- Metaphors **don't** use the words **like** or **as.**

- Metaphors are like similes because they compare things that aren't really alike.
- How is a metaphor different from a simile? (Idea: *It doesn't use **like** or **as.**)*
- That's right. A metaphor doesn't say that one thing is **like** another thing. It says that one thing **is** another thing.

- Listen. Here's a simile: **In a crisis, Fritz is like a rock.** Here's a metaphor: **In a crisis, Fritz is a rock.**
- What do the simile and metaphor both compare? (Idea: *Fritz and a rock.*)
- Both the simile and metaphor compare Fritz to a rock. Both let us know Fritz is steady, and he'll be there in a crisis.
- How are the simile and metaphor different? (Idea: *The metaphor doesn't use **like** or **as.**)*
- In the simile, Fritz is **like** a rock. In the metaphor, he **is** a rock.

2. Listen: **Marlene is her sister's puppet.**
- It that a simile or metaphor? (Signal.) *Metaphor.*
- What two things does it compare? (Idea: *Marlene and a puppet.*)
- How are they alike? (Ideas: *Both are controlled by someone else; both do what someone else wants them to do.*) ✔

3. Look at your worksheet for lesson 93. ✔

4. You're going to answer the questions about each metaphor. Use your dictionary for help. Raise your hand when you've finished.

   (Observe students and give feedback.)

5. (After students complete the items, do a workcheck. For each item, call on a student to answer the questions. If the answer is wrong, say the correct answer.)

Answer Key: 1. the tornado and an angry child **2. Ideas:** They both toss things around; they both destroy things around them. **3.** Marley and an encyclopedia **4. Idea:** Both are full of information. **5.** Our classroom and a freezer **6. Idea:** Both are very cold.

Materials: Each student will need a copy of the worksheet for lesson 94 (Blackline Master 94); the teacher and each student will need a copy of the same children's dictionary.

EXERCISE 1
METAPHORS

Name _____

94

Lesson 94

A. Answer the questions about each metaphor. Use your dictionary.

The Wrestling Wild Man is a mountain!

1. What two things are compared? _____

2. How are they similar? _____

When she dances, Katerina is a feather in the wind.

3. What two things are compared? _____

4. How are they similar? _____

The pond is a mirror.

5. What two things are compared? _____

6. How are they similar? _____

B. Write S next to each simile and M next to each metaphor.

1. _____ Kimba is a swan.
2. _____ Your smile is the sun to me.
3. _____ Pete is as sharp as a tack.
4. _____ My tractor runs like a deer.

BLM 94 239

1. What the name for expressions that compare things without using the words **like** or **as**? (Signal.) *Metaphors.*
2. Find part A on your worksheet. ✔
3. You're going to answer the questions about each metaphor. Use your dictionary for help. Raise your hand when you've finished.
   (Observe students and give feedback.)
4. (After students complete the items, do a workcheck. For each item, call on a student to answer the questions. If the answer is wrong, say the correct answer.)

Answer Key: 1. Wrestling Wild Man and a mountain **2. Idea:** Both are very large.

3. Katrina and a feather **4. Ideas:** Both are very light; both sway and move gracefully.
5. The pond and a mirror **6. Ideas:** Both can reflect images; both are smooth.

EXERCISE 2

FIGURES OF SPEECH

1. Let's review figures of speech.
- What are **figures of speech**? (Idea: *Expressions that speakers and writers use when they want us to picture something clearly in our minds.*)
- What are two figures of speech that compare things that aren't really alike? (Idea: *Similes and metaphors.*)
- How is a metaphor different from a simile? (Idea: *It doesn't use **like** or **as**.*)
2. Listen: **My friend Art is a computer.** Is that a simile or metaphor? (Signal.) *Metaphor.*
- Yes, it says that Art **is** a computer. It means that Art can make a lot of calculations very fast.
- How can you make it into a simile? (Idea: *Add **like** or **as**.*)
- What's the simile? (Idea: *My friend Art is like a computer.*)
3. Find part B on your worksheet. ✔
- Write **S** next to each simile and **M** next to each metaphor. Raise your hand when you've finished.
4. (After students complete the items, do a workcheck. For each item, call on a student to say it if is a simile or metaphor. If the answer is wrong, say the correct answer.)

Answer Key: 1. metaphor **2.** metaphor **3.** simile **4.** simile

Lesson 95

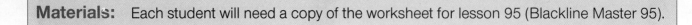

Materials: Each student will need a copy of the worksheet for lesson 95 (Blackline Master 95).

PERSONIFICATION

> **95**
> **Lesson 95**
> Name _____
>
> * **Personification** is a kind of expression that describes nonliving things as humans.
> * Nonliving things described as humans are **personified.**
>
> **Answer the questions about each personification.**
>
> **As she opened the door, the icy wind slapped Tori in the face.**
>
> 1. What is being personified? _____
> 2. How is it personified? _____
>   _____
>
> **The stars winked at me.**
>
> 3. What is being personified? _____
> 4. How is it personified? _____
>
> **The rosebuds smiled up at us from the garden.**
>
> 5. What is being personified? _____
> 6. How is it personified? _____
>   _____
>
> 240 BLM 95

1. Find your worksheet for lesson 95. ✔
* You're going to learn about another kind of figure of speech: **personification.** You say it. (Signal.) *Personification.*
* Follow along as I read what's in the box:

> * **Personification** is a kind of expression that describes nonliving things as humans.
>
> * Nonliving things described as humans are **personified.**
---

2. Here's an example of personification: **As the children played, the sun wrapped them warmly in his arms.**
* What's being personified? (Signal.) *The sun.*

* How is the sun personified? (Ideas: *He has arms; he can wrap his arms around the children.*)
* Does the sun have arms? (Signal.) *No.*
* No, the sun has rays. When children play in the sun's rays, it might look like the rays are wrapping around them like arms. Using personification makes the sentence more interesting.
3. Here's another example of personification: **After a long bout of coughing, the car finally died.**
* What's being personified? (Idea: *A car.*)
* How is it being personified? (Ideas: *It has a mouth and lungs and can cough; it is alive and can die.*)
* Can a car really cough or die like a human? (Signal.) *No.*
* No, it's just a more interesting way to tell about a car that's not working right.
4. You're going to answer the questions about each personification. Raise your hand when you've finished.
(Observe students and give feedback.)
5. (After students complete the items, do a workcheck. For each item, call on a student to answer the questions. If the answer is wrong, say the correct answer.)

Answer Key: 1. The icy wind **2. Idea:** It has hands and can slap. **3.** Stars **4. Idea:** They have eyes and can wink. **5.** Rosebuds **6. Idea:** They have mouths and can smile.

Materials: Each student will need a copy of the worksheet for lesson 96 (Blackline Master 96).

EXERCISE 1
PERSONIFICATION

> 96
>
> Name _____
> Lesson 96
>
> **A. Answer the questions about each personification.**
>
> **The tree branch grabbed Billy's shirt.**
>
> 1. What is being personified? _____
>
> 2. How is it personified? _____
> _____
>
> **The campfire spit sparks at the ranger.**
>
> 3. What is being personified? _____
>
> 4. How is it personified? _____
> _____
>
> **B. Fill in the circle next to the kind of figure of speech that is used in the sentence.**
>
> 1. The moon was as bright as a lantern.
>   ○ simile   ○ metaphor   ○ personification
> 2. Larry is dynamite.
>   ○ simile   ○ metaphor   ○ personification
> 3. I'm a chicken when it comes to rock climbing.
>   ○ simile   ○ metaphor   ○ personification
> 4. The sofa invited me to take a nap.
>   ○ simile   ○ metaphor   ○ personification
> 5. In that shirt, you'll stand out like a sore thumb.
>   ○ simile   ○ metaphor   ○ personification
>
> BLM 96   241

1. What kind of figure of speech describes nonliving things as humans? (Signal.) *Personification.*
2. Find part A for lesson 96. ✔
- Answer the questions about each personification. Raise your hand when you've finished.
  (Observe students and give feedback.)
3. (After students complete the items, do a workcheck. For each item, call on a student to answer the questions. If it is wrong, say the correct answer.)

Answer Key: 1. The tree branch **2. Idea:** It has hands and can grab. **3.** Campfire **4. Idea:** It has a mouth and can spit.

EXERCISE 2
FIGURES OF SPEECH

1. Let's review figures of speech.
- What are figures of speech? (Idea: *Expressions that speakers and writers use when they want us to picture something clearly in our minds.*)
- What are the two figures of speech compare things that aren't really alike? (Idea: *Similes and metaphors.*)
- How is a metaphor different from a simile? (Idea: *It doesn't use **like** or **as.***)
- What figure of speech describes nonliving things as humans, or persons? (Signal.) *Personification.*
- **The angry mountain threw tons of snow down on the climbers.** What kind of figure of speech is that? (Signal.) *Personification.*
- **The cat was a stone statue.** What kind of figure of speech? (Signal.) *Metaphor.*
- **The cat was as still as a stone statue.** What kind of figure of speech? (Signal.) *Simile.*
2. Find part B on your worksheet. ✔
- Fill in the circle next to the kind of figure of speech that is used in the sentence. Raise your hand when you've finished.
  (Observe students and give feedback.)
3. (After students complete the items, do a workcheck. For each item, call on a student to give the answer. If the answer is wrong, say the correct answer.)

Answer Key: 1. simile **2.** metaphor **3.** metaphor **4.** personification **5.** simile

Lesson 97

IDIOMS

97
Lesson 97

Name _____

Write what each idiom really means.

1. The school's new gym cost an arm and a leg to build.

_____

2. After winning the contest, Alice was walking on air.

_____

3. I get cold feet every time I have to talk to the class.

_____

4. After spilling the soup in my lap, the waiter said my lunch was on the house.

_____

5. I hope you'll drop me a line after you move.

_____

242 BLM 97

1. Some expressions speakers and writers use don't mean exactly what the words say. These expressions are called **idioms.** You say it. (Signal.) *Idioms.*

- Speakers and writers use idioms to make things more interesting.

2. Here's an example of an idiom: **She's afraid of her own shadow.** Does that really mean her own shadow frightens her? (Signal.) *No.*

- What does it mean? (Ideas: *She's easily frightened; she's a coward.*)

3. Here's another example: **Jon's head is always in the clouds.**

- Does that really mean that Jon's so tall his head sticks up into the clouds? (Signal.) *No.*

- What does it mean? (Ideas: *He's a dreamer; he doesn't pay attention to what's around him; his mind is always somewhere else.*)

4. Look at your worksheet for lesson 97. ✔

- Write what each idiom really means. Raise your hand when you've finished. (Observe students and give feedback.)

5. (After students complete the items, do a workcheck. For each item, call on a student to give the answer. If the answer is wrong, say the correct answer.)

Answer Key: Ideas: 1. It cost a lot. **2.** She was happy. **3.** I get afraid; I get nervous. **4.** Lunch was free. **5.** Write to me.

EXERCISE 1
IDIOMS

98

Name _____
Lesson 98

Write what each idiom really means.

1. Money just burns a hole in Brent's pocket.
   _____
2. It's raining cats and dogs.
   _____
3. Cassie and Polly stole the show with their dancing.
   _____
4. Jimmy looks down in the dumps.
   _____

B. **Fill in the circle next to the kind of figure of speech that is used in the sentence.**

1. The dish washer grumbled and groaned, but it washed the big load of dishes.
   ○ simile   ○ metaphor   ○ personification
2. My computer is a dinosaur.
   ○ simile   ○ metaphor   ○ personification
3. I'm as hungry as a bear.
   ○ simile   ○ metaphor   ○ personification
4. The blowing trash danced and skipped down the street.
   ○ simile   ○ metaphor   ○ personification

BLM 98 243

1. What's the name for expressions that don't mean exactly what the words say? (Signal.) *Idioms.*
2. Listen: **Wanda has a green thumb when it comes to growing tomatoes.** Does that really mean that Wanda's thumb is green? (Signal.) *No.*
- What does it mean? (Ideas: *She's good at growing tomatoes; she has a lot of luck growing tomatoes.*)
3. Find part A on your worksheet for lesson 98. ✔

- Write what each idiom really means. Raise your hand when you've finished. (Observe students and give feedback.)
4. (After students complete the items, do a workcheck. For each item, call on a student to give the answer. If the answer is wrong, say the correct answer.)

Answer Key: Ideas: 1. Brent spends money fast; he doesn't keep money very long. **2.** It's raining very hard. **3.** They were the highlight of the show; they were the center of attention. **4.** He's unhappy; he's depressed.

EXERCISE 2
FIGURES OF SPEECH

1. Find part B on your worksheet. ✔
- Each sentence uses a figure of speech. It can be a simile, metaphor, or personification.
- Fill in the circle next to the kind of figure of speech that is used in the sentence. Raise your hand when you've finished.
2. (After students complete the items, do a workcheck. For each item, call on a student to give the answer. If the answer is wrong, say the correct answer.)

Answer Key: 1. personification
2. metaphor **3.** simile **4.** personification

Lesson 99

Materials: Each student will need a copy of the worksheet for lesson 99 (Blackline Master 99).

SEMICOLONS

99

Lesson 99

Name _____

- **Semicolons (;)** are used in writing to show longer pauses than commas.
- **Semicolons** can be used to join two complete thoughts in compound sentences.
- When semicolons are used in **compound sentences,** they take the place of commas and conjunctions.

Rewrite the sentences. Put semicolons where they belong.

1. I have information about three summer camps I can't tell which one is best.

   _____

2. Look at that sunset I've never seen anything so beautiful.

   _____

3. Mr. Garza is a great Spanish teacher he grew up in Mexico.

   _____

4. E. B. White was a great writer he wrote *Charlotte's Web.*

   _____

5. Vonda called me yesterday she wanted to go to skating.

   _____

244 BLM 99

1. Find your worksheet for lesson 99. ✔
- You know that commas are punctuation marks used in writing to show readers where to pause in a sentence. Now let's talk about another kind of punctuation mark: **semicolons.**
- Follow along as I read what's in the box:

  - **Semicolons (;)** are used in writing to show longer pauses than commas.
  - **Semicolons** can be used to join two complete thoughts in compound sentences.
  - When semicolons are used in **compound sentences,** they take the place of commas and conjunctions.

2. (Write on the board:)

   1. **Martin went to the planetarium, and Allen went to the aquarium.**
   2. **Martin went to the planetarium; Allen went to the aquarium.**

- Look at sentence 1: **Martin went to the planetarium, and Allen went to the aquarium.**
- It has two complete thoughts. How are the two thoughts joined? (Idea: *With a comma and the conjunction **and.***)
- Sentence 2: **Martin went to the planetarium; Allen went to the aquarium.**
- This sentence also has two complete thoughts. How are they joined? (Idea: *With a semicolon.*)

3. You're going to rewrite sentences and put semicolons where they belong. Raise your hand when you've finished. (Observe students and give feedback.)

4. (After students complete the items, do a workcheck. Call on a student to read each rewritten sentence, saying "semicolon" to indicate where a semicolon is needed. If the answer is wrong, say the correct answer.)

Answer Key:
1. I have information about three summer camps; I can't tell which one is best.
2. Look at that sunset; I've never seen anything so beautiful.
3. Mr. Garza is a great Spanish teacher; he grew up in Mexico.
4. E. B. White was a great writer; he wrote *Charlotte's Web.*
5. Vonda called me yesterday; she wanted to go to skating.

Materials: Each student will need a copy of the worksheet for lesson 100 (Blackline Master 100).

SEMICOLONS

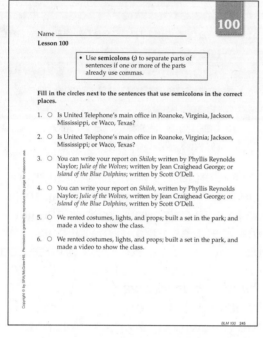

1. Find your worksheet for lesson 100. ✔
- Here's some more information about semicolons. Follow along as I read:

> • Use **semicolons (;)** to separate parts of sentences if one or more of the parts already use commas.

2. (Write on the board:)

> 1. **Scott brought soda; Dawn brought chips, salsa, and dip; and Kevin brought napkins.**
> 2. **Her favorite books are *Sounder*, which is by William Armstrong; *Owl Moon*, which is by Jane Yolen; and *Corduroy*, which is by Don Freeman.**
> 3. **We traveled to Boise, Idaho; Boulder, Colorado; and Bismarck, North Dakota.**

- Sentence 1 has three parts. The first part is **Scott brought soda.** The second part is **Dawn brought chips, salsa, and dip.** The third part is **Kevin brought napkins.**
- The second part already uses commas. So do you use more commas to separate the three parts in the sentence? (Signal.) *No.*
- What punctuation marks do you use? (Signal.) *Semicolons.*
- Sentence 2: **Her favorite books are *Sounder*, which is by William Armstrong; *Owl Moon*, which is by Jane Yolen; and *Corduroy*, which is by Don Freeman.**
- The sentence lists the names of three books and their authors. Each part of the sentence already uses a comma, so you use semicolons to separate the two parts.
- Sentence 3: **We traveled to Boise, Idaho; Boulder, Colorado; and Bismarck, North Dakota.**
- This sentence names three places. In each place name, the cities and states are separated by commas. So how are the three place names separated from each other in the sentence? (Signal.) *With semicolons.*
3. Fill in the circles next to the sentences that use semicolons in the correct places. Raise your hand when you've finished.

(Observe students and give feedback.)

Answer Key: The correct sentences are **2, 4,** and **5.**

Lesson 101

Materials: Each student will need a copy of the worksheet for lesson 101 (Blackline Master 101).

COLONS

101
Lesson 101

Name _____

- **Colons (:)** direct reader's attention to what a writer wants to highlight.
- When a sentence contains words and phrases such as **these, the following,** or **as follows,** use colons to introduce **a list of items.**
- **Don't** use colons to introduce a list of items if the list follows a verb or preposition.

Rewrite only the sentences that **don't** use colons correctly. You'll put colons in some sentences and take them out of others. If a sentence is correct, write **correct.**

1. Mom's grocery list contained these items: milk, bread, and juice.

2. I send e-mails to: Charlie, Derek, Phoebe, and Kirsten.

3. My schedule includes the following classes art, math, science, reading, social studies, and music.

4. The sports I like best are hockey, skating, and wrestling.

246 BLM 101

1. You know about commas and semicolons. Now let's talk about another kind of punctuation mark: **colons.**
2. Find your worksheet for lesson 101. ✔
- Here's some information about colons. Follow along as I read:

> - **Colons (:)** direct reader's attention to what a writer wants to highlight.
>
> - When a sentence contains words and phrases such as **these, the following,** or **as follows,** use colons to introduce **a list of items.**
>
> - **Don't** use colons to introduce a list of items if the list follows a verb or preposition.

3. (Write on the board:)

> 1. **The experiment requires these materials: magnets, sand, and metal bars.**
> 2. **The materials for the experiment include magnets, sand, and metal bars.**
> 3. **I sent a list of the materials to Arnie, Angelina, and Ed.**

- In Sentence 1, I want to call attention to the materials needed for an experiment, so I use a colon to introduce the list: **magnets, sand, and metal bars.** I also use the word **these.** What phrase could I have used in place of **these**? (Ideas: *The following; as follows.*)
- That's right: **The experiment requires the following materials: magnets, sand, and metal bars.**
- Look at Sentence 2: **The materials for the experiment include magnets, sand, and metal bars.** Does it have a list of items? (Signal.) *Yes.*
- Is the list introduced by a colon? (Signal.) *No.*
- What word comes before the list? (Signal.) *Include.*
- What part of speech is **include**? (Signal.) *A verb.*
- What's the rule? (Idea: *Don't use a colon if the list follows a verb.*)
- Sentence 3: **I sent a list of the materials to Arnie, Angelina, and Ed.**
- Is the list introduced by a colon? (Signal.) *No.*
- What word comes before the list? (Signal.) *To.*

- What part of speech is **to**? (Signal.) *A preposition.*
- What's the rule? (Idea: *Don't use a colon if the list follows a preposition.*)
4. You're going to rewrite the sentences that don't use colons correctly. You'll put colons in some sentences and take them out of others. If a sentence is correct, write **correct**. Raise your hand when you've finished.
  (Observe students and give feedback.)
5. (After students complete the items, do a workcheck. For each item, call on a student to say whether it uses a colon correctly. Have the student read each rewritten sentence, saying "colon" to indicate where a colon is needed. If the answer is wrong, say the correct answer.)

Answer Key:
1. (correct)
2. I send e-mails to Charlie, Derek, Phoebe, and Kirsten.
3. My schedule includes the following classes: art, math, science, reading, social studies, and music.
4. (correct)

Lesson 102

SEMICOLONS AND COLONS

Name _____

Lesson 102

102

Fill in the circles next to the sentences that use semicolons and colons in the correct places.

1. ○ Please check to see that you have these things: paper, pencil, test booklet, and dictionary.

2. ○ Please check to see that you have these things; paper, pencil, test booklet, and dictionary.

3. ○ Please check to see that you have these things paper, pencil, test booklet, and dictionary.

4. ○ We need to: mop the floors; dust the desk, tables, and shelves; and wash all of the windows.

5. ○ We need to mop the floors; dust the desk, tables, and shelves; and wash all of the windows.

6. ○ We need to mop the floors: dust the desk, tables, and shelves: and wash all of the windows.

7. ○ Zander wants to see you he has a plan for the project.

8. ○ Zander wants to see you: he has a plan for the project.

9. ○ Zander wants to see you; he has a plan for the project.

BLM 102   247

1. What's the name for the punctuation mark that shows longer pauses than a comma? (Signal.) *Semicolon.*

- When do you use semicolons? (Ideas: *To join two complete thoughts in a compound sentence; to separate parts of sentences if one or more parts already use commas.*)

- What's the name for the punctuation mark that directs readers' attention to what writers want to highlight? (Signal.) *Colon.*

- When do you use colons? (Idea: *To introduce a list of items in a sentence.*)

- Do you always use colons to introduce lists? (Signal.) *No.*

- No, you use a colon if a sentence contains words and phrases such as **these, the following,** or **as follows.**

- You **don't** use colons to introduce a list of items if the list follows what parts of speech? (Ideas: *Verbs or prepositions.*)

2. Find your worksheet for lesson 102. ✔

- You're going to fill in the circles next to the sentences that use semicolons and colons correctly. Raise your hand when you've finished.
  (Observe students and give feedback.)

3. (After students complete the items, do a workcheck. Call on a student to read each sentence, then say whether and why it's correct or incorrect. If the answer is wrong, say the correct answer.)

Answer Key: The correct sentences are **1, 5,** and **9.**

Materials: Each student will need a copy of the worksheet for lesson 103 (Blackline Master 103).

QUOTATION MARKS IN DIRECT QUOTATIONS

103
Lesson 103   Name _____

> • **Quotation marks (" ")** are always used in pairs. They highlight the words that come between them.
> • Use quotation marks around the **exact words** that somebody says or writes. The exact words are called a **quotation**.
> • Begin quotations with **capital letters.** Put periods **inside** the closing quotation marks.
> • If they're part of the quotation, put **question marks** and **exclamation points inside** the closing quotation marks.
> • If they're part of the sentence but not the quotation, put **question marks** and **exclamation points outside** the closing quotation marks.
> • Use **commas** to set off words such as **he said** or **she asks** from the quotation.

Fill in the circles next to the sentences that use quotation marks and other punctuation marks correctly. Look at the information in the box for help.

1. ○ "Dad said, Take these clothes to the cleaners."
2. ○ Dad said, "Take these clothes to the cleaners."
3. ○ George asked, "Which way to the depot?"
4. ○ George asked "Which way to the depot?"
5. ○ Do you remember who said, "A penny for your thoughts?"
6. ○ Do you remember who said, "A penny for your thoughts"?

248 _BLM 103_

1. Find your worksheet for lesson 103. ✔
- Here's some information about **quotation marks.** Follow along:

> - **Quotation marks (" ")** are always used in pairs. They highlight the words that come between them.
> - Use quotation marks around the **exact words** that somebody says or writes. The exact words are called a **quotation.**
> - Begin quotations with **capital letters.** Put periods **inside** the closing quotation marks.
> - If they're part of the quotation, put **question marks** and **exclamation points inside** the closing quotation marks.

> - If they're part of the sentence but not the quotation, put **question marks** and **exclamation points outside** the closing quotation marks.
> - Use **commas** to set off words such as **he said** or **she asks** from the quotation.

2. (Write on the board:)

> 1. Eunice asked, "Who cleaned up?"
> 2. Did you hear me say "Let's clean up"?

- Look at sentence 1. What are Eunice's exact words? (Idea: *Who cleaned up?*)
- So quotations marks go before **Who** and after and **Who** begins with a capital letter. Is the question mark inside or outside the closing quotation marks? (Signal.) *Inside.*
- Eunice asked a question the question mark is part of the quotation.
- Is the comma before or after the opening quotation marks? (Signal.) *Before.*
- Sentence 2: **Did you hear me say "Let's clean up the playground"?**
- The quotations marks go before **Let's** and after **playground.** Is the question mark inside or outside the closing quotation marks? (Signal.) *Outside.*
- This time it's the complete sentence, not just the quotation, that's a question.

3. Fill in the circles next to the sentences that use quotation marks and other punctuation marks correctly. Raise your hand when you've finished.
(Observe students and give feedback.)

Answer Key: The correct sentences are **2, 3,** and **6.**

Lesson 104

QUOTATION MARKS

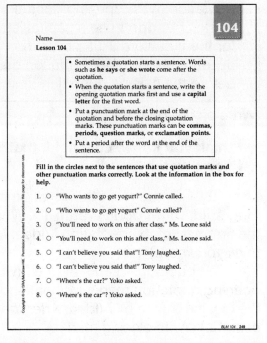

1. Find your worksheet for lesson 104. ✔
- Here's some more information about quotation marks. Follow along:

> - Sometimes a quotation starts a sentence. Words such as **he says** come after the quotation.
> - When the quotation starts a sentence, write the opening quotation marks first and use a **capital letter** for the first word.
> - Put a punctuation mark at the end of the quotation and before the closing quotation marks. These punctuation marks can be **commas, periods, question marks,** or **exclamation points.**
> - Put a period after the word at the end of the sentence.

2. (Write on the board:)

> 1. **"It's time for your medicine,"** **Owen said.**
> 2. **"Watch out for that pothole!"** **Tom yelled.**

- Look at sentence 1: **"It's time for your medicine," Owen said.** What are Owen's exact words? (Idea: *It's time for your medicine.*)
- The quotations marks start the sentence, and **It's** begins with a capital letter.
- What punctuation mark is at the end of the quotation? (Signal.) *A comma.*
- Is the comma inside or outside the closing quotation marks? (Signal.) *Inside.*
- What punctuation mark is at the end of the sentence? (Signal.) *A period.*
- Sentence 2: **"Watch out for that pothole!" Tom yelled.**
- The quotations marks go before **Watch** and after **pothole.** Is the exclamation point inside or outside the closing quotation marks? (Signal.) *Inside.*
- Yes, the quotation is an exclamation, so the mark goes inside the quotation marks. The period goes at the end of the sentence.
3. You're going to fill in the circles next to the sentences that use quotation marks and other punctuation marks correctly. Look at the information in the box for help. Raise your hand when you've finished.

(Observe students and give feedback.)

Answer Key: The correct sentences are **1, 4, 6,** and **7.**

Lesson 105

Materials: Each student will need a copy of the worksheet for lesson 105 (Blackline Master 105).

QUOTATION MARKS

105

Lesson 105

Name _____

- Sometimes a quotation is split in a sentence. Part of it comes before words such as **he says** or **she called** and part of it comes after.
- When the quotation is split, put quotation marks at the beginning and at the end of each part.
- For the first part, write opening quotation marks and use a capital letter for the first word. Put a comma before the closing quotation marks.
- Put a comma after the words that tell who said the quotation.
- For the second part of the quotation, write opening quotation marks, but **don't** use a capital letter for the first word. Put a period, question mark, or exclamation point before the closing quotation marks.

Fill in the circles next to the sentences that use quotation marks and other punctuation marks correctly. Look at the information in the box for help.

1. ○ "I heard," Mac said. "That Chuck is moving."
2. ○ "I heard," Mac said, "that Chuck is moving."
3. ○ "If you don't hurry." Carolyn called, "we'll be late."
4. ○ "If you don't hurry," Carolyn called, "we'll be late."
5. ○ "Just wait a minute," Donna laughed, "and the weather will change."
6. ○ "Just wait a minute, Donna laughed, and the weather will change."

250   BLM 105

1. Find your worksheet for lesson 105. ✔
- Here's some more information about how to use quotation marks.

- Sometimes a quotation is split in a sentence. Part of it comes before expressions such as **he says** or **she called** and part of it comes after.

- When the quotation is split, put quotation marks at the beginning and at the end of each part.

- For the first part, write opening quotation marks and use a capital letter for the first word. Put a comma before the closing quotation marks.

- Put a comma after the words that tell who said the quotation.

- For the second part of the quotation, write opening quotation marks, but **don't** use a capital letter for the first word. Put a period, question mark, or exclamation point before the closing quotation marks.

2. (Write on the board:)

I think you know, Ling said, that I don't watch TV.

- Look at the sentence: **I think you know, Ling said, that I don't watch TV.** What's the first part of the quotation? (Idea: *I think you know.*)
- We need quotation marks before **I** (write opening quotation marks.) Where should the closing marks be? (Idea: *After the comma.*) (Write closing marks.)
- Who said the quotation? (Signal.) *Ling.*
- Does **Ling said** have quotation marks? (Signal.) *No.*
- What punctuation mark follows those words? (Signal.) *A comma.*
- What's the last part of the quotation? (Idea: *That I don't watch TV.*)
- We need quotation marks before **that** (Write opening marks.) Does **that** begin with a capital letter? (Signal.) *No.*
- Where should the closing marks be? (Idea: *After the period.*) (Write closing quotation marks.)

3. It's your turn. Fill in the circles next to the sentences that use quotation marks and other punctuation marks correctly. Raise your hand when you've finished. (Observe students and give feedback.)

Answer Key: The correct sentences are **2, 4,** and **5.**

Materials: Each student will need a copy of the worksheet for lesson 106 (Blackline Master 106).

HYPHENS

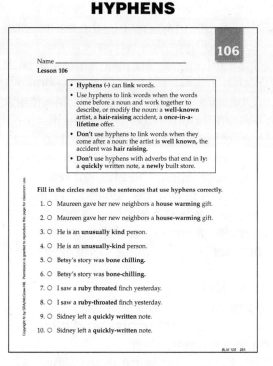

1. Find your worksheet for lesson 106. ✔
- Let's talk about another kind of punctuation mark: **hyphens.**
- Here's some information about hyphens. Follow along as I read:

> - **Hyphens (-)** can **link** words.
>
> - Use hyphens to link words when the words come before a noun and work together to describe, or modify the noun: a **well-known** artist, a **hair-raising** accident, a **once-in-a-lifetime** offer.
>
> - **Don't** use hyphens to link words when they come after a noun: the artist is **well known,** the accident was **hair raising.**

> - **Don't** use hyphens with adverbs that end in **ly:** a **quickly** written note, a **newly** built store.

2. (Write on the board:)

> 1. **Henry wore a lemon yellow jacket.**
> 2. **Henry's jacket was lemon yellow.**
> 3. **It was a bitterly cold morning.**

- Look at Sentence 1: **Henry wore a lemon yellow jacket.** What words describe **jacket**? (Signal.) *Lemon yellow.*
- Does **lemon-yellow** need a hyphen? (Signal.) *Yes.*
- Why do the words need a hyphen? (Idea: *Because they work together to describe jacket, and they come before jacket.*)
- Sentence 2: **Henry's jacket was lemon yellow.** Does **lemon yellow** need a hyphen here? (Signal.) *No.*
- Why don't the words need a hyphen? (Idea: *Because lemon yellow comes after jacket.*)
- Sentence 3: **It was a bitterly cold morning.** What words describe **morning**? (Signal.) *Bitterly cold.*
- Should **bitterly cold** have a hyphen? (Signal.) *No.*
- Why not? The words come before the noun. (Idea: *Because you don't use hyphens with adverbs that end in ly.*)
3. Fill in the circles next to the sentences that use hyphens correctly. Raise your hand when you've finished. (Observe students and give feedback.)

Answer Key: The correct sentences are **2, 3, 5, 8,** and **9.**

Lesson 107

HYPHENS

107

Lesson 107

Name _____

Rewrite only the sentences that **don't** use hyphens correctly. You'll put in some hyphens and take some out. If a sentence is correct, write **correct.**

1. Warren wore a sky-blue suit and shoes that were snow white.

2. We were caught unprepared by the rapidly-moving storm.

3. Did you see those ruby red slippers?

4. The McCall family's dogs are always well-behaved.

5. Barbara has become a well-known poet.

6. Alex asked for an up or down vote.

7. I stared sadly at the completely-flat tire.

252 BLM 107

1. Let's review when to use hyphens.
- Use hyphens to link words when the words come before a noun and work together to describe the noun.
- **Don't** use hyphens to link words when they come after a noun.
- **Don't** use hyphens with adverbs that end in **ly.**

2. Find your worksheet for lesson 107. ✔
3. You're going to rewrite the sentences and add hyphens where they're needed. If a sentence is correct, write **correct.** Raise your hand when you've finished. (Observe students and give feedback.)
4. (After students complete the items, do a workcheck. Call on a student to say whether each sentence is correct or incorrect. Have the student read each rewritten sentence, saying "hyphen" to indicate when a hyphen is needed. If the answer is wrong, say the correct answer.)

Answer Key:
1. (correct)
2. We were caught unprepared by the rapidly moving storm.
3. Did you see those ruby-red slippers?
4. The McCall family's dogs are always well behaved.
5. (correct)
6. Alex asked for an up-or-down vote.
7. I stared sadly at the completely flat tire.

Lesson 108

Materials: Each student will need a copy of the worksheet for lesson 108 (Blackline Master 108).

FACT VS. OPINION

Name _____

Lesson 108

- **Facts** are statements that can be proved. Facts can be proved with the following:
  —**statistics,** or numbers
  —**examples**
- **Opinions** are personal beliefs or feelings. Opinions **can't** be proved.

Write **fact** if the statement can be proved. Write **opinion** if it's just a feeling or belief that can't be proved.

1. _____ Last year, teenagers bought more than 20 million CDs.
2. _____ Most of the CDs teenagers buy are just loud noise.
3. _____ The average CD costs about fifteen dollars.
4. _____ Some CDs cost as much as thirty dollars.
5. _____ No CD is worth thirty dollars!
6. _____ Music on CDs is better than the music on old vinyl records.
7. _____ CDs weren't available thirty years ago.

BLM 108 253

1. Find your worksheet for lesson 108. ✔
- Follow along as I read what's in the box:

> - **Facts** are statements that can be proved. Facts can be proved with the following:
>   —**statistics,** or numbers
>   —**examples**
> - **Opinions** are personal beliefs or feelings. Opinions **can't** be proved.

- What do we call statements that can be proved with statistics or examples? (Signal.) *Facts.*
- What are personal beliefs or feelings that can't be proved? (Signal.) *Opinions.*
- Listen: **The Great Wall of China is more than 1,400 miles long.** Is that statement a fact or opinion? (Signal.) *Fact.*

- Yes, you can prove the statement by measuring the Great Wall of China, so it's a fact.
- Listen: **The Great Wall of China is the greatest human achievement of all time.** Is that statement a fact or opinion? (Signal.) *Opinion.*
- It's an opinion because you can't prove the statement. It's just a feeling or belief.

2. Look at the statements. You're going to write **fact** if the statement can be proved and **opinion** if it's just a feeling or belief that can't be proved.
- Statement 1: **Last year, teenagers bought more than 20 million CDs.**
- Is that a fact or an opinion? (Signal.) *Fact.*
- Why is it a fact? (Idea: *It can be proved by checking the number.*)
- Statement 2: **Most of the CDs teenagers buy are just loud noise.**
- Is that a fact or an opinion? (Signal.) *Opinion.*
- Why is it an opinion? (Ideas: *It can't be proved; it's just a feeling or belief.*)
- Do the rest of the items. Raise your hand when you've finished.
  (Observe students and give feedback.)

3. (After the students complete the items, do a workcheck. For each item, call on a student to read the sentence and say if it is a fact or opinion. Ask the student to tell why the item is a fact or opinion. If the answer is wrong, say the correct answer.)

Answer Key: 1. fact **2.** opinion **3.** fact **4.** fact **5.** opinion **6.** opinion **7.** fact

Lesson 109

Materials: Each student will need a copy of the worksheet for lesson 109 (Blackline Master 109).

FACT VS. OPINION

1. Let's review.
- What are statements that can be proved? (Signal.) *Facts.*
- What personal beliefs or feelings that can't be proved? (Signal.) *Opinions.*
2. Find your worksheet for lesson 109. ✔
- Follow along as I read:

> There's no better place to live than Charleston, West Virginia. Charleston is the capital of West Virginia. It's the prettiest state capital in the United States. Charleston is located in the Allegheny Mountains. The hiking trails in the Alleghenies are much better than those in the Rockies. The views from the mountains can't be beat. Charleston is also near the Elk and Kanawha rivers. The people in Charleston are the friendliest in the country.

3. Some of the sentences in the paragraph state facts and some give opinions.
- Look at the numbered sentences below the box.
- Sentence 1: **There's no better place to live than Charleston, West Virginia.** Is that a fact or an opinion? (Signal.) *Opinion.*
- Yes, it's a belief that can't be proved.
- Look at sentence 2: **Charleston is the capital of West Virginia.** Is that a fact or an opinion? (Signal.) *Fact.*
- That's a statement you can prove.
4. Finish the sentences. Write **fact** if the statement can be proved. Write **opinion** if it's just a feeling or belief that can't be proved. Raise your hand when you've finished.
   (Observe students and give feedback.)
5. (After the students complete the items, do a workcheck. For each item, call on a student to read the sentence and say if it is a fact or opinion. Ask the student to tell why the item is a fact or opinion. If the answer is wrong, say the correct answer.)

Answer Key: 1. opinion **2.** fact **3.** opinion **4.** fact **5.** opinion **6.** opinion **7.** fact **8.** opinion

Materials: Each student will need a copy of the worksheet for lesson 110 (Blackline Master 110).

TIME AND ORDER WORDS AND EXPRESSIONS

Name _____
Lesson 110

110

Time Words and Expressions
today, tomorrow, yesterday, last month, next year, this morning, ago, once, now, past
Order Words and Expressions
after, at first, at last, before, during, finally, first, later, last, next, second, then, third

A. Circle the words in each paragraph that signal time or order.

1. Ana decided to make a cake. The first thing she did was find the flour, eggs, and sugar. The second thing she did was locate the cake pan. The third thing she did was mix the batter. Then she put the cake in the oven. The last thing Ana did was eat the cake.

2. I visited my cousins last month; next week I'll visit my great-grandpop. I hope I can visit Aunt Flo later.

B. Write two paragraphs. In the first, use time words and expressions from the box to signal when something happened. In the second paragraph, use order words and expressions from the box to signal the order in which things happen.

_____
_____
_____
_____
_____
_____

BLM 110 255

1. Time and order words and expressions connect ideas in writing. They help readers follow the development of events.
- **Time words and expressions** signal when things happen.
- **Order words and expressions** signal which things come before and which come after.
2. Find your worksheet for lesson 110. ✔
- The box contains some words and expressions that signal **time.** Follow along as I read them:

Time Words and Expressions

today, tomorrow, yesterday, last month, next year, this morning, ago, once, now, past

- (Write on the board:)

Yesterday Nicole painted the basement. Today she papered her room. Tomorrow she'll work on her sister's room.

- The paragraph tells when three things happened. What word signals when Nicole painted the basement? (Signal.) *Yesterday.*
- What word signals when she papered her room? (Signal.) *Today.*
- What word signals when she'll work on her sister's room? (Signal.) *Tomorrow.*
3. Look at your worksheet again. The box also contains some words and expressions that signal **order.** Follow along as I read them:

Order Words and Expressions

after, at first, at last, before, during, final, finally, first, later, last, next, now, second, then, third

- (Write on the board:)

Myron worked on his report all day. First he found the books he needed. Then he read for two hours. Next he took notes. Finally he wrote the report.

- The paragraph tells the order in which four things happened. What word signals the first thing Myron did? (Signal.) *First.*
- What word signals the second thing he did? (Signal.) *Then.*
- What word signals the third thing? (Signal.) *Next.*

- What word signals the last thing Myron did? (Signal.) *Finally.*

4. Find part A on your worksheet. ✔

- Circle the words in each paragraph that signal time or order. Raise your hand when you've finished.
  (Observe students and give feedback.)

5. (After the students complete the items, do a workcheck. Call on a student to tell the words circled in each paragraph. If the answer is wrong, say the correct answer.)

Answer Key: (Part A:) The following words should be circled in the paragraphs: 1. first, second, third, Then, last **2.** last month, next week, later

6. Now find part B on your worksheet. ✔

- Write two paragraphs. In the first, use time words and expressions from the box to show when something happened. In the second paragraph, use order words and expressions from the box to show the order in which things happen. Raise your hand when you've finished.

7. (After the students finish, call on them to read their paragraphs. Then have them say each time or order signal used. Accept paragraphs that use signals correctly.)

Materials: Each student will need a copy of the worksheet for lesson 111 (Blackline Master 111).

LOCATION WORDS AND EXPRESSIONS

> **111**
>
> Name _____
>
> Lesson 111
>
> **Location Words and Expressions**
> above, across, around, beside, behind, between, in, in front of, in back of, inside, near, next to, on, outside, over, straight ahead, through, under, right, left, up, down
>
> **A. Circle the words in each paragraph that signal location.**
>
> 1. Greg walked through the door of his mother's office. She sat behind her desk, frowning. In front of her on the desk was Greg's report card.
>
> 2. When you enter the woods, walk straight ahead for about a mile. You'll come to two paths. Take the path on your left. Go between the two big rocks, and you'll see a stream. Follow it down to the falls. Our cabin is next to the falls.
>
> **B. Write a paragraph. Use location words and expressions from the box to signal where something is.**
>
> _____
> _____
> _____
> _____
> _____
> _____
> _____
> _____
>
> 256 BLM 111

1. **Time and order signals** connect ideas in writing by showing when things happen and which things come before and which come after.
- What are some time signals? (Ideas: *Today; tomorrow; yesterday; last month; next year; ago; once; past.*)
- What are some order signals? (Ideas: *After; at first; at last; before; during; finally; first; later; last; next; second; then; third.*)
2. Find your worksheet for lesson 111. ✔
- Let's talk about another kind of signal words and expressions. They signal **location.**
- **Location signals** connect ideas in writing by helping readers get a clearer picture of where things happen.

- The box contains some location signals. Follow along as I read them:

> **Location Words and Expressions**
>
> above, across, around, beside, behind, between, in, in front of, in back of, inside, near, next to, on, outside, over, straight ahead, through, under, right, left, up, down

3. Find part A on your worksheet. ✔
- Circle the words in each paragraph that signal location. Raise your hand when you've finished.
  (Observe students and give feedback.)
4. (After the students complete the items, do a workcheck. Call on a student to tell the words circled in each paragraph. If the answer is wrong, say the correct answer.)

Answer Key: (Part A:) The following words should be circled in the paragraphs:
1. through, behind, In front of **2.** straight ahead, left, between, down, next to

5. Now find part B on your worksheet. ✔
- Write a paragraph. Use location words and expressions from the box to show where something is. Raise your hand when you've finished.
6. (After the students finish, call on them to read their paragraphs. Then have them say each location signal used. Accept paragraphs that use the signals correctly.)

Lesson 112

WORDS AND EXPRESSIONS THAT SIGNAL CHANGE

1. You know about words that connect ideas in writing by signaling time, order, and location. Now let's talk about some words and expressions that connect ideas by letting you know that something is changing.

2. Find your worksheet for lesson 112. ✔

- The box contains some words and expressions that signal changes. Follow along as I read them:

> **Words and Expressions That Signal Change**
>
> although, but, however, instead, on the other hand, otherwise, rather, yet

3. Find part A on your worksheet. ✔

- Circle the words in each paragraph that signal changes. Raise your hand when you've finished.
  (Observe students and give feedback.)

4. (After the students complete the items, do a workcheck. Call on a student to tell the words circled in each paragraph. If the answer is wrong, say the correct answer.)

Answer Key: (Part A:) The following words should be circled in the paragraphs: **1.** Instead, On the other hand, **2.** although, however, Rather

5. Now find part B on your worksheet. ✔

- Write a paragraph. Use words and expressions from the box to signal change. Raise your hand when you've finished.

6. (After the students finish, call on them to read their paragraphs. Then have them say each signal used. Accept paragraphs that use the signals correctly.)

Materials: Each student will need a copy of the worksheet for lesson 113 (Blackline Master 113).

CAUSE-AND-EFFECT RELATIONSHIPS

113

Lesson 113

Name _____

Words That Signal Cause-and-Effect Relationships
because, so, therefore

Answer the questions about each cause-and-effect relationship.

The boat hit a rock; therefore, it had to be repaired.

1. What happened? _____
2. What caused it to happen? _____
3. What word signals the relationship between what happened and what caused it to happen? _____

Ivy twisted her ankle, so she lost the race.

4. What happened? _____
5. What caused it to happen? _____
6. What word signals the relationship between what happened and what caused it to happen? _____

Cassidy took a summer job because he wanted to earn money.

7. What happened? _____
8. What caused it to happen? _____
9. What word signals the relationship between what happened and what caused it to happen? _____

258   BLM 113

1. Let's talk about some words that signal the relationship between what happens and what causes it to happen.
- The name for this relationship is **cause and effect.**
2. Find your worksheet for lesson 113. ✔
- The box contains some words that signal cause-and-effect relationships. Follow along as I read them:

> **Words That Signal Cause-and-Effect Relationships**
>
> because, so, therefore

- (Write on the board:)

> 1. **The picture was blurry because Bonita moved the camera.**
> 2. **Burt overslept, so he missed the bus.**
> 3. **Burt missed the bus; therefore, he had to walk.**

- Look at sentence 1: **The picture was blurry because Bonita moved the camera.**
- What happened? (Idea: *The picture was blurry.*)
- What caused the picture to be blurry? (Idea: *Bonita moved the camera.*)
- What word signals the relationship between what happened and what caused it to happen? (Signal.) *Because.*
- What's the name for that relationship? (Signal.) *Cause and effect.*
- Sentence 2: **Burt overslept, so he missed the bus.**
- What happened? (Idea: *Burt missed the bus.*)
- What caused him to miss the bus? (Idea: *He overslept.*)
- What word signals the relationship between what happened and what caused it to happen? (Signal.) *So.*
- Sentence 3: **Burt missed the bus; therefore, he had to walk.**
- What happened? (Idea: *Burt had to walk.*)
- What caused that to happen? (Idea: *He missed the bus.*)
- What word signals the relationship between what happened and what caused it to happen? (Signal.) *Therefore.*

3. Look at your worksheet. ✔
   Answer the questions about each cause-
   and-effect relationship. Raise your hand
   when you've finished.
   (Observe students and give feedback.)

Answer Key: 1. The boat had to be repaired
2. It hit a rock **3.** therefore **4.** Ivy lost the
race **5.** She twisted her ankle **6.** so
7. Cassidy took a summer job **8.** He wanted
to earn money **9.** because

Materials: Each student will need a copy of the worksheet for lesson 114 (Blackline Master 114).

FIXING RUN-ON SENTENCES

Name _____

Lesson 114

- A **run-on sentence** is two or more sentences that are combined with conjunctions.
- To correct a run-on sentence, rewrite it as two or more separate sentences.

Rewrite each run-on sentence as two or more separate sentences. Don't use any conjunctions. Remember to start each sentence with a capital letter and end it with a period.

1. We went to the fair and we rode the rides and we had popcorn.

2. Mr. Marcelli made the posters and Tricia decorated the room and Benny took the tickets.

3. The village is more than five hundred years old but it is in the mountains and it is hard to get to but it is beautiful.

BLM 114   259

Copyright © by SRA/McGraw-Hill. Permission is granted to reproduce this page for classroom use.

1. Look at your worksheet for lesson 114. ✔
- The box contains some information about run-on sentences. Follow along as I read:

> - A **run-on sentence** is two or more sentences that are combined with conjunctions.
>
> - To correct a run-on sentence, rewrite it as two or more separate sentences.

2. Look at the first sentence: **We went to the fair and we rode the rides and we had popcorn.**
- That's really three separate sentences: **We went to the fair. We rode the rides. We had popcorn.**
- Write the sentences. Start each sentence with a capital letter and end it with a period. Raise your hand when you've finished.
  (Observe students and give feedback.)
3. Now read sentence 2 and rewrite it as two or more separate sentences. Don't use any conjunctions. Remember to start each sentence with a capital letter and end it with a period. Raise your hand when you've finished.
  (Observe students and give feedback.)
4. Here's what you should have:
  Capital M. Mr. Marcelli made the posters. Period.
  Capital T. Trica decorated the room. Period.
  Capital B. Benny took the tickets. Period.
5. If you got anything wrong, fix it.
6. **(Repeat for item 3.)**

Lesson 115

Materials: Each student will need a copy of the worksheet for lesson 115 (Blackline Master 115).

FIXING RUN-ON SENTENCES

115

Lesson 115   Name _____

Rewrite each run-on sentence as two or more separate sentences. Don't use any conjunctions. Remember to start each sentence with a capital letter and end it with a period.

1. We were surprised to get a package and we tore it open but it was just a video ad from a toothpaste company.

_____
_____
_____

2. Mildred hoped her book would be read by students and she hoped it would be made into a movie but she never thought it would win a prize.

_____
_____
_____

3. Tim had to outline the project and he had to find the camera and he had to take the pictures but he finished everything on time.

_____
_____
_____

260 BLM 115

---

1. What's the name for a sentence that's really two or more sentences combined with conjunctions? (Signal.) *Run-on sentence.*

- How can you correct a run-on sentence? (Idea: *Rewrite it as two or more separate sentences.*)

2. Look at your worksheet for lesson 115. ✔

- Rewrite each run-on sentences as two or more separate sentences. Don't use any conjunctions. Remember to start each sentence with a capital letter and end it with a period.

3. Read item 1, then rewrite it. Raise your hand when you've finished. (Observe students and give feedback.)

- Here's what you should have:
  Capital W. We were surprised to get a package. Period.
  Capital W. We tore it open. Period.
  Capital I. It was just a video ad from a toothpaste company. Period.

- If you got anything wrong, fix it.

4. (Repeat for items 2 and 3.)

| Materials: | Each student will need a copy of the worksheet for lesson 116 (Blackline Master 116). |

FIXING UNCLEAR SENTENCES

> 116
>
> Name _____
> Lesson 116
>
> **In the yard, the boys saw a dog.**
>
> Picture A   Picture B
>
> Rewrite the sentence so that it tells about Picture A.
>
> _____
> _____
> _____
>
> Rewrite the sentence so that it tells about Picture B.
>
> _____
> _____
> _____
>
> BLM 116 261

1. In earlier lessons, you worked with parts of speech called **prepositions** and about groups of words called **prepositional phrases.** Let's review.
- **Prepositions** are words that relate nouns or pronouns to other words in a sentence.
- What are some common prepositions? (Ideas: *About; after; around; before; behind; between; by; from; in; near; of; off; over; through.*)
- A **prepositional phrase** is a group of words that begins with a preposition and ends with a noun or pronoun. It tells us more about where something is located.
- Here are some prepositional phrases: **In the house, by the river, near it, behind them, off the chart, after the play.**
- If a prepositional phrase is not put in the right place, it can make the meaning of a sentence unclear.

2. Find your worksheet for lesson 116. ✔

A   B

- Look at the sentence: **In the yard, the boys saw a dog.**
- The meaning of the sentence isn't clear. It can mean that the boys were in the yard and saw a dog. It can also mean that the boys saw a dog that was in the yard. We can't tell whose location the prepositional phrase is telling about, the boys or a dog.
- Look at picture A. What's in the yard? (Signal.) *The boys.*
- Write a sentence that tells about picture A. Put the prepositional phrase right after the word it tells about. Raise your hand when you've finished.
  (Observe students and give feedback.)
- (Write on the board:)

> **The boys in the yard saw a dog.**

- In picture A, the boys are in the yard, so you put the phrase **in the yard** right after the word **boys.** Here's what you should have. Fix any mistakes.
3. Look at picture B. What's in the yard? (Signal.) *A dog.*

- Write a sentence that tells about this picture. Raise your hand when you've finished.

  (Observe students and give feedback.)
- (Write on the board:)

  > **The boys saw a dog in the yard.**

- In picture B, the dog is in the yard, so you put the phrase **in the yard** right after the word **dog.** Here's what you should have. Fix any mistakes.

Materials: Each student will need a copy of the worksheet for lesson 117 (Blackline Master 117).

FIXING UNCLEAR SENTENCES

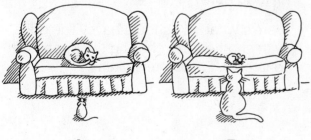

1. Remember, if a prepositional phrase is not put in the right place, it can make the meaning of a sentence unclear.
2. Find your worksheet for lesson 117. ✔

- Look at the sentence: **The cat saw the mouse.** You're going to rewrite that sentence. You'll put the prepositional phrase **on the sofa** in the right place so that it tells about either picture A or picture B.
- Write the sentence for picture A. Raise your hand when you've finished. (Observe students and give feedback.)
- (Write on the board:)

> **The cat on the sofa saw the mouse.**

- Here's what you should have. The cat is on the sofa, so you put the phrase **on the sofa** right after the word **cat.** Fix any mistakes.
3. Write the sentence for picture B. Raise your hand when you've finished. (Observe students and give feedback.)
- (Write on the board:)

> **The cat saw the mouse on the sofa.**

- Here's what you should have. In picture B, the mouse is on the sofa, so you put the phrase **on the sofa** right after the word **mouse.** Fix any mistakes.

Lesson 118

FIXING UNCLEAR SENTENCES

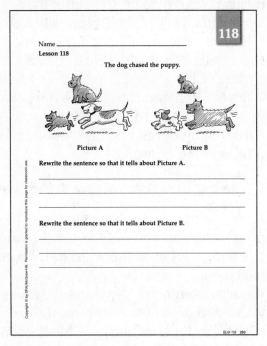

1. Remember, if a prepositional phrase is not put in the right place, it can make the meaning of a sentence unclear.
2. Find your worksheet for lesson 118. ✔

- Look at the sentence: **The dog chased the puppy.** You're going to rewrite that sentence. You'll put the prepositional phrase **with long ears** in the right place so that it tells about either picture A or picture B.
- Write the sentence for picture A. Raise your hand when you've finished. (Observe students and give feedback.)
- (Write on the board:)

> **The dog with long ears chased the puppy.**

- Here's what you should have. The dog with long ears is chasing the puppy with short ears, so you put the phrase **with long ears** right after the word **dog.** Fix any mistakes.
3. Write the sentence for picture B. Raise your hand when you've finished. (Observe students and give feedback.)
- (Write on the board:)

> **The dog chased the puppy with long ears.**

- Here's what you should have. The dog with short ears is chasing the puppy with long ears. Fix any mistakes.

Materials: Each student will need a copy of the worksheet for lesson 119 (Blackline Master 119).

FIXING UNCLEAR SENTENCES

119
Lesson 119

Name _____

Our street has tall buildings and trees.

Picture A   Picture B

Rewrite the sentence so that it tells about Picture A.

_____

_____

Rewrite the sentence so that it tells about Picture B.

_____

_____

264 BLM 119

1. You worked with adjectives in earlier lessons. Let's review.
- What are **adjectives**? (Idea: *Words that describe nouns or pronouns.*)
- You know that prepositional phrases need to be in the right place to make the meaning of a sentence clear. The same thing is true for adjectives.
2. (Write on the board:)

> **1. The cats have blue eyes and collars.**

- What's the adjective in sentence 1? (Signal.) *Blue.*
- The meaning of that sentence isn't clear. **Blue** might be describing both the eyes and the collars of the cats.

(Write on the board:)

> **2. The cats have blue eyes and blue collars.**

- Sentence 2 makes the meaning clear by using the adjective twice—once for each noun it describes.
- Sentence 1 might also mean that the cats have blue eyes and that they are wearing collars. The collars might be red or green or brown.
- (Write on the board:)

> **3. The cats have collars and blue eyes.**

- Sentence 3 makes the meaning clear by moving **collar** first and using **blue** only with **eyes,** the noun it describes.
3. Find your worksheet for lesson 119. ✔

A   B

- Follow along as I read the sentence: **Our street has tall buildings and trees.**
- What's the adjective? (Signal.) *Tall.*
- The meaning of the sentence is not clear. **Tall** might be describing both the buildings and the trees. Or it might be describing just the buildings.

4. Look at picture A. Rewrite the sentence so that it tells about that picture.
- Raise your hand when you've finished. **(Observe students and give feedback.)**
- **(Write on the board:)**

> **Our street has tall buildings and tall trees.**

- Here's what you should have. Putting **tall** before both **buildings** and **trees** makes the sentence mean that the street has **both** tall buildings and tall trees. Fix any mistakes.

5. Rewrite the sentence for picture B. Raise your hand when you've finished. **(Observe students and give feedback.)**
- **(Write on the board:)**

> **Our street has trees and tall buildings.**

- Here's what you should have. This makes the meaning clear by moving **trees** first and using **tall** to describe only **buildings**. Fix any mistakes.

Materials: Each student will need a copy of the worksheet for lesson 120 (Blackline Master 120).

FIXING UNCLEAR SENTENCES

Name _____

Lesson 120

The store sells old books and newspapers.

Picture A   Picture B

Rewrite the sentence so that it tells about picture A.

_____

_____

Rewrite the sentence so that it tells about picture B.

_____

_____

BLM 120   265

1. Find your worksheet for lesson 120. ✔

A   B

- Follow along as I read the sentence: **The store sells old books and newspapers.**
- What's the adjective? **(Signal.)** *Old.*
- The meaning of the sentence is not clear. **Old** might be describing both the books and the newspapers. Or it might be describing just the books.
2. Look at picture A. Rewrite the sentence so that it tells about that picture.
- Raise your hand when you've finished. **(Observe students and give feedback.)**
- (Write on the board:)

The store sells old books and newspapers .

- Here's what you should have. Putting **old** before both **books** and **newspapers** makes the sentence mean that the store sells **both** old books and newspapers. Fix any mistakes.
3. Rewrite the sentence for picture B. Raise your hand when you've finished. **(Observe students and give feedback.)**
- (Write on the board:)

The store sells newspapers and old books.

- Here's what you should have. This makes the meaning clear by moving **newspapers** first and using **old** to describe only **books**. Fix any mistakes.

Name _____

Lesson 1

A.

Table of Contents		
Lesson	**Selection**	**Page**
1	A Trip through Time	2
2	The Golden Fleece	12
3	Sally and the Salamander	16
4	The Magic Lantern	22
5	Grandfather's Story	38
6	The View from Mars	50
7	Stars and Planets	62
8	A New Home for Jessie	86

B. Write the answer to each question.

1. What part of a book shows a list of the selections in the book?

   _____

2. What is the title of the selection for lesson 3?

   _____

3. On what page does the selection for lesson 3 begin?

   _____

4. What is the title of the selection for lesson 7?

   _____

5. On what page does that selection begin?

   _____

6. What is the name of the selection that begins on page 22?

   _____

Name _____

Lesson 2

> ### Index
> Algeria, 352, 355
> Apollo space program, 270, 274
> Aztec calendar, 450–453
> Bacon, Roger, 340
> Bartók, Béla, 116–119
> bats, 339–344
> Brazil, 71, 89
> computers, 139–143
>   development of, 130
>   parts of, 140
>   programs, 143
>   uses for, 140–142
> daylight savings time, 87, 129
> Doppler radar, 222, 274, 412

B. Write the answer to each question.

1. What is the number of the first page in the book that tells about Brazil?

    _____

2. What is the number of the first page in the book that tells about Doppler radar?

    _____

3. What topic can you find out about on page 129?

    _____

4. What pages in the book tell about computers?

    _____

5. On what page can you find out about the parts of a computer?

    _____

6. What is the number of the last page in the book that tells about Béla Bartók?

    _____

3

Name _____

Lesson 3

A.

famished	gallant

f

famished When you are *famished*, you are very, very hungry.

fat People used to use *fat* to fry food. Today, most people use cooking oil instead of fat.

fawn A *fawn* is a young deer.

feeble Something that is very weak is *feeble*.

fit When somebody has a *fit*, that person loses consciousness and may writhe around.

flask A *flask* is a king of bottle.

flee When you *flee*, you move as fast as you can.

fleece The fur of a sheep is called, *fleece*.

flinch When you *flinch*, you jump when somebody startles you.

fret When you worry about something, you *fret* about that thing.

frivolous Someone who is foolish and not serious is *frivolous*.

fulfill When something is *fulfilled*, that thing comes true.

furnish When you supply something, you *furnish* it.

g

gadget Another word for a *device* is a *gadget*.

gale A *gale* is a terrible storm with great winds.

gallant Somebody who is very brave and noble is *gallant*.

B. Look at the guide words for each page. Write the page number for each word.

page 171	gratify	inlet
page 172	insecure	jamboree
page 173	jealousy	lurk

1. intricate _____

2. lobby _____

3. hobble _____

4. isolate _____

5. kettle _____

6. jostle _____

7. idle _____

Name _____

Lesson 4

For each item, write the name of the part of the book that you would use. The answer to each item is table of contents, index, or glossary.

1. You want to find out what reading selection starts on page 202.

   _____

2. You want to find out on what page the book first discusses malaria.

   _____

3. You want to find out the meaning of the word **cataclysm.**

   _____

4. You want to find out the name of the reading selection for lesson 14.

   _____

5. You want to find out the page number for the fifth selection in the book.

   _____

6. You want to find out the first page number for the topic **television.**

   _____

7. You want to find out if the word **noble** has more than one meaning in the book.

   _____

Name _____

Lesson 5

Use your dictionary to find the meaning of each word. Circle the correct meaning.

1. **suppress**   The governor tried to <u>suppress</u> information about her fund raising.

   • find out   • hold back   • organize

2. **tedious**   The speaker gave a <u>tedious</u> explanation of how to forecast weather.

   • interesting   • detailed   • boring

3. **concise**   Your report should be <u>concise</u>.

   • brief   • accurate   • good

4. **adversary**   Why do you treat me like an <u>adversary</u>?

   • child   • enemy   • servant

5. **dwindle**   We saw our food supply <u>dwindle</u> each day.

   • decrease   • rot   • increase

6. **merge**   The two companies agreed to <u>merge</u>.

   • close   • meet   • combine

Name _____

Lesson 6

Use your dictionary to find the meaning of each word. Circle the correct meaning.

1. **whippet**   Mary's <u>whippet</u> won a ribbon at the county fair.
   - dog   - flower   - dessert

2. **detest**   I <u>detest</u> carrots.
   - like   - hate   - grow

3. **grovel**   We will not <u>grovel</u> for your attention.
   - beg   - yell   - search

4. **ketch**   Jen spent all afternoon on her <u>ketch</u>.
   - front porch   - computer   boat

5. **intimidate** Don't try to <u>intimidate</u> us.
   - arrest   - frighten   - find

6. **truculent**   Trudy is a <u>truculent</u> child.
   - pretty   - mean   - quiet

7

Name _____

Lesson 7

Use your dictionary to find the correct meaning of the underlined word in each sentence. Circle the correct meaning.

1. The new library building is <u>immense</u>.

   • huge   • empty   • ugly

2. The company decided to <u>launch</u> its new car models at the national auto show.

   • sell   • introduce   • drive

3. Don't be so <u>insolent</u>.

   • slow   • stubborn   • rude

4. After they entered the theme park, Fred wanted to <u>elude</u> his big brothers.

   • get money from   • get away from   • get food for

5. The writer of the book is <u>anonymous</u>.

   • famous   • rich   • unknown

6. The students decided to <u>defy</u> the school dress code.

   • disobey   • rewrite   • keep

7. Your plan to paint the room purple is <u>absurd</u>!

   • silly   • thoughtful   • interesting

Name _____

Lesson 8

Use an encyclopedia to answer these questions.

1. In what year was President John F. Kennedy born?

    _____

2. Who was the first woman prime minister of Israel?

    _____

3. What kind of government does Sweden have?

    _____

4. What was the country of Kampuchea once known as?

    _____

5. When was the satellite Sputnik launched into space?

    _____

6. What kind of animals are bats?

    _____

Name _____

Lesson 9

Use an encyclopedia to answer these questions.

1. In what country is the volcano Krakatoa located?

    _____

2. What is the average life span of a killer whale?

    _____

3. Who was Euripides?

    _____

4. What are some good sources of vitamin A?

    _____

5. What is the state bird of Hawaii?

    _____

6. In what year did Catherine the Great become empress of Russia?

    _____

Name _____

Lesson 10

Use an encyclopedia to answer these questions.

1. What is the capital city of Ukraine?

   _____

2. In what year was the treaty signed that ended the American
   Revolutionary War?

   _____

3. What is the name of Upton Sinclair's best known book?

   _____

4. Who was the first president of the American Federation of Labor?

   _____

5. For whom was the state of Georgia named?

   _____

6. Who was Sally K. Ride?

   _____

7. What is President Ronald W. Reagan's middle name?

   _____

Name _____

Lesson 11

Use the United States atlas to answer these questions.

1. Which state is directly north of Kansas?

_____

2. What's the capital city of Louisiana?

_____

3. What's the name of the tallest mountain in Connecticut?

_____

4. What lake is near Oshkosh, Wisconsin?

_____

5. Which one of the following cities is in the western part of Arkansas: Little Rock, Pine Bluff, or Fort Smith?

_____

6. What large body of water is near Seattle, Washington?

_____

Name _____

Lesson 12

Use the world atlas to answer these questions.

1. What is the capital city of India?

    _____

2. Which one of the following countries touches Finland: Poland, Russia, or Denmark?

    _____

3. What country forms the southern border of Paraguay?

    _____

4. What is the major river in Mali?

    _____

5. What large body of water is the eastern border of Saudi Arabia?

    _____

6. The country of Tibet is located in what chain of mountains?

    _____

13

Name _____

Lesson 13

Write atlas, dictionary, or encyclopedia to tell the resource that you would use to find the information.

1. How far is it from Norfolk, Virginia to Baltimore, Maryland?

    _____

2. What is the major religion of Somalia?

    _____

3. What does the word **lachrymose** mean?

    _____

4. Which city is closest to Oneida Lake in New York: Albany, Utica, or Syracuse?

    _____

5. In what year was hockey's Stanley Cup first awarded?

    _____

6. What two oceans touch Australia?

    _____

7. In what year was Herman Melville born?

    _____

8. Which word means "unfeeling or cold": **callus** or **callous**?

    _____

Name _____

Lesson 14

Write the word that means the opposite for each word on the list.

1. **agree**   _____

2. **connect**   _____

3. **appear**   _____

4. **like**   _____

5. **satisfied**   _____

6. **honor**   _____

7. **order**   _____

8. **prove**   _____

9. **allow**   _____

Name _____

A. Write the word with the prefix that means **again**.

1. tie _____

2. sell _____

3. play _____

4. charge _____

5. group _____

B. Write words with the prefixes **dis** and **re**

	dis	re
1. locate	_____	_____
2. appear	_____	_____
3. connect	_____	_____
4. assemble	_____	_____
5. arm	_____	_____
6. mount	_____	_____

Name _____

Lesson 16

A. Write the word with the prefix that means not.

1. **comfortable** _____

2. **ready** _____

3. **reliable** _____

4. **met** _____

5. **talented** _____

B. Write the word that answers the question. The word you write will have one of these prefixes: dis, re, or un.

1. What word means **the opposite of qualified?** _____

2. What word means **not natural?** _____

3. What word means **to direct again?** _____

4. What word means **to invent again?** _____

5. What word means **the opposite of believe?** _____

6. What word means **not scientific?** _____

17

Name _____

Lesson 17

A. Write the word with the prefix that means before.

1. writing _____

2. determine _____

3. school _____

4. trial _____

5. order _____

B. Circle the correct word. Use your dictionary to check your answers.

1. Jason and Jordan look alike, but they have very **dissimilar, unsimilar** personalities.

2. Our TV show is so popular, we will **prebroadcast, rebroadcast** it three more times.

3. As Paul sped down the long hill, his bike chain came **disattached, unattached.**

4. It's a good idea to **preplan, replan** for college while you're in high school.

Name _____

Lesson 18

Write the word with the prefix that means not. Use your dictionary to check your answers.

1. **prepared** _____

2. **sane** _____

3. **justice** _____

4. **helpful** _____

5. **accurate** _____

6. **imaginable** _____

7. **gracious** _____

8. **human** _____

9. **exact** _____

Name _____

Lesson 19

A. Write a word with the prefix that means **many** to complete each sentence.

1. **national**   The president attended a _____ conference.

2. **media**   The _____ concert was broadcast over TV, radio, and the Internet.

3. **lane**   The state plans to build a _____ highway near our home.

4. **cultural**   Our school has a wide choice of _____ courses.

5. **stage**   The trip to Mars required the use of a _____ rocket.

B. Write the word that answers the question. The word you write will have one of these prefixes: **dis, re, un, pre, in,** or **multi.** Use your dictionary to check your answers.

1. What word means **not known**?   _____

2. What word means **the opposite of honor**?   _____

3. What word means **to decorate again**?   _____

4. What word means **not convenient**?   _____

5. What word means **many units**?   _____

6. What word means **to pay before**?   _____

Name _____

Lesson 20

A. Write a word that means very or more than to complete each sentence

1. **strong**   The weightlifter was _____.

2. **power**   The United States is a _____.

3. **human**   To win the race took a _____ effort.

4. **rich**   Only the _____ can afford to live here.

5. **charged**   Greg's car has a _____ engine.

B. Circle the correct word. Use your dictionary to check your answers.

1. The hotel towels are **multisoft, supersoft.**

2. The noise was so loud, it was absolutely **unbearable, disbearable.**

3. We **prearranged, unarranged** our trip to Mexico almost a year ago.

4. After falling at the starting block, the runner got up and **preentered, reentered** the race.

5. You can't **disprove, unprove** what I told you.

6. The town doesn't need another **multistory, superstory** building.

7. The cab driver took the most **indirect, undirect** way to the airport.

Name _____

Lesson 21

Write the word with the suffix that means **without**.

1. weight _____

2. effort _____

3. age _____

4. shape _____

5. home _____

6. clue _____

7. color _____

8. sound _____

9. worth _____

Name _____

Lesson 22

Write the word with the suffix that means **full of** to complete the sentence.

1. **cheer**   The good news made us feel _____.

2. **color**   The autumn leaves are quite _____.

3. **peace**   The sleeping cat looks very _____.

4. **play**   The _____ puppies nipped at my toes.

5. **help**   Thank you for being so _____.

6. **grace**   The _____ dancers swept across the floor.

B. Write the word that answers the question. Write the word using one of the prefixes listed in the box. Use your dictionary to check your answers.

> **Prefixes:** dis, re, un, pre,
> in, multi, super

1. What word means **before the war**?   _____

2. What word means **not healthy**?   _____

3. What word means **to build again**?   _____

4. What word means **the opposite of loyal**?   _____

5. What word means **not valid**?   _____

6. What word means **more than a store**?   _____

7. What word means **many regions**?   _____

23

Name _____

Lesson 23

A. Write the word with the suffix that means being.

1. cold _____

2. smooth _____

3. mean _____

4. weak _____

5. good _____

B. Write the word that answers the question. Write the word using one of the suffixes you've learned. Use your dictionary to check your answers.

1. What word means **without a name?** _____

2. What word means **full of shame?** _____

3. What word means **without motion?** _____

4. What word means **being bold?** _____

5. What word means **full of doubt?** _____

6. What word means **full of meaning?** _____

7. What word means **being smug?** _____

Name _____

Lesson 24

A. Write the word with the suffix that means one who to complete the sentence.

1. **read**   Benny is an avid _____.

2. **pitch**   Who wants to be the _____ for the first ball game?

3. **send**   I wrote "return to _____" on the letter and dropped it in the mailbox.

4. **lead**   James is the _____ of our new club.

5. **design**   Samantha's dress was made especially for her by a world-famous clothing _____.

B. Write the word that answers the question. Write the word using one of the prefixes or suffixes you've learned. Use your dictionary to check your answers.

1. What word means **not kind**?   _____

2. What word means **to view before**?   _____

3. What word means **full of respect**?   _____

4. What word means **not decisive**?   _____

5. What word means **one who prints**?   _____

6. What word means **without harm**?   _____

7. What word means **being tough**?   _____

8. What word means **the opposite of allow**?   _____

Name _____

Lesson 25

A. **Write the word with the suffix that means can be.** Use your dictionary to check your spelling.

1. **read**   _____

2. **approach**   _____

3. **exhaust**   _____

4. **express**   _____

5. **trace**   _____

B. **Use what you know about prefixes and suffixes to answer each question. Use your dictionary.**

1. What does the word **uneven** mean?

   _____

2. What does the word **evenness** mean?

   _____

3. What does the word **unknown** mean?

   _____

4. What does the word **knowable** mean?

   _____

5. What does the word **discomfort** mean?

   _____

6. What does the word **blissful** mean?

   _____

7. What does the word **fighter** mean?

   _____

Name _____

Lesson 26

A. Write the word with the suffix that means **in a certain way** to complete the sentence.

1. **quick**   Barb walked _____ to the park.

2. **brief**   Hank paused _____ before he entered the room.

3. **extreme**   José was _____ upset when you didn't call him.

4. **active**   Harriet is _____ involved in several community groups.

5. **sweet**   The children sang _____.

B. Write the word that answers the question. Write the word using one of the prefixes or suffixes you've learned. Use your dictionary to check your answers.

1. What word means **in a faint way**?   _____

2. What word means **one who dances**?   _____

3. What word means **full of power**?   _____

4. What word means **being small**?   _____

5. What word means **without end**?   _____

6. What word means **can be reversed**?   _____

7. What word means **to cut before**?   _____

8. What word means **the opposite of claim**? _____

9. What word means **without humor**?   _____

10. What word means **can be replaced**?   _____

Name _____

Lesson 27

Underline the prefix, circle the root, and draw a line over the suffix. Then write the meaning of the word. Use your dictionary.

1. **disprove**

Meaning: _____

2. **changeable**

Meaning: _____

3. **untruthful**

Meaning: _____

4. **infrequently**

Meaning: _____

5. **nearness**

Meaning: _____

6. **pretrial**

Meaning: _____

7. **gatherer**

Meaning: _____

8. **close**

Meaning: _____

Name _____

Lesson 28

Underline the prefix, circle the root, and draw a line over the suffix. Then write the meaning of the word. Use your dictionary.

1. **shyness**

Meaning: _____

2. **guiltless**

Meaning: _____

3. **indirectly**

Meaning: _____

4. **unskillful**

Meaning: _____

5. **reoccur**

Meaning: _____

6. **briskly**

Meaning: _____

7. **multimedia**

Meaning: _____

Name _____

Lesson 29

ROOTS			
aud	hear	**dict**	speak, tell
cred	believe	**vis**	see

Use the information in the box and what you've learned about prefixes and suffixes to write the meanings of the words.

1. **audible**

Meaning: _____

2. **inaudible**

Meaning: _____

3. **predictable**

Meaning: _____

4. **visible**

Meaning: _____

5. **invisible**

Meaning: _____

6. **credible**

Meaning: _____

7. **incredible**

Meaning: _____

Name _____

Lesson 30

ROOTS			
equi	equal	**port**	carry
flex	bend	**volv**	turn, roll

Use the information in the box and what you've learned about prefixes and suffixes to write the meanings of the words.

1. **flexible**

Meaning: _____

2. **inflexible**

Meaning: _____

3. **revolve**

Meaning: _____

4. **portable**

Meaning: _____

5. **porter**

Meaning: _____

6. **equitable**

Meaning: _____

7. **inequitable**

Meaning: _____

Name _____

Lesson 31

Use your dictionary to find the meanings of the homographs. Write two meanings for each word.

A. light

1. _____

2. _____

B. train

3. _____

4. _____

C. tick

5. _____

6. _____

D. down

7. _____

8. _____

E. hail

9. _____

10. _____

Name _____

Lesson 32

Use your dictionary to find the meanings of the homographs. Write two meanings for each word.

A. sock

1. _____

2. _____

B. palm

3. _____

4. _____

C. well

5. _____

6. _____

D. lean

7. _____

8. _____

E. stern

9. _____

10. _____

33

Lesson 33

Use your dictionary to find the meanings of the homographs. Write two sentences for each word. Use a different meaning of the word in each sentence.

A. top

1. _____

2. _____

B. yard

3. _____

4. _____

C. ring

5. _____

6. _____

D. present

7. _____

8. _____

Name _____

Lesson 34

Write a sentence for each homophone in a set. Use your dictionary.

1. **board** _____

_____

2. **bored** _____

_____

3. **feat** _____

_____

4. **feet** _____

_____

5. **grate** _____

_____

6. **great** _____

_____

7. **cereal** _____

_____

8. **serial** _____

_____

Name _____

Lesson 35

Write a sentence for each homophone in a set. Use your dictionary.

1. **cell** _____

   _____

2. **sell** _____

   _____

3. **fair** _____

   _____

4. **fare** _____

   _____

5. **dew** _____

   _____

6. **due** _____

   _____

7. **loan** _____

   _____

8. **lone** _____

   _____

Name _____

Lesson 36

Write a sentence for each homophone in a set. Use your dictionary.

1. **principal** _____

    _____

2. **principle** _____

    _____

3. **hair** _____

    _____

4. **hare** _____

    _____

5. **oar** _____

    _____

6. **ore** _____

    _____

7. **plain** _____

    _____

8. **plane** _____

    _____

37

Name _____

Lesson 37

> • Begin the first word of every sentence with a capital letter.
> • Begin the names of people, ethnic groups, places, organizations, languages, religions, and nationalities with capital letters.

If a word should begin with a capital letter, underline the letter.

1. please don't interrupt the speaker.

2. Our new neighbors are jeb and patsy ryan.

3. Michelle is french, but she speaks italian and english.

4. The new german teacher is from mobile, alabama.

5. the organization for applied technology held its meeting in freeport, maine, this year.

6. our library has a large collection of native american literature.

Name _____

Lesson 38

> - Begin the names of the days of the week with capital letters.
> - Begin the names of months with capital letters.
> - **Don't** begin the names of the seasons with capital letters.
> - **Don't** begin the names of words used to show directions with capital letters.

If a sentence doesn't use capital letters correctly, rewrite it. If it uses capital letters correctly, write correct.

1. Mitch visits his friend every tuesday.

_____

2. We usually take our vacation in june.

_____

3. Each Spring, we plant new trees.

_____

4. Colorado is North of New Mexico and West of Kansas.

_____

5. Molly, Jeb, and Cindy were all born in April.

_____

39

Name _____

Lesson 39

If a sentence doesn't use capital letters correctly, rewrite it. If it uses capital letters correctly, write correct.

1. Corrina lives just south of the county line.

   _____

2. do you know the way to san jose?

   _____

3. I can't remember if your birthday is in march or april.

   _____

4. larry is a member of scientists for the public interest.

   _____

5. The program was supported by Catholics, Jews, and Muslims.

   _____

6. Martin is african american, and kim is asian american.

   _____

7. my favorite time of year is winter.

   _____

Name _____

Lesson 40

If Sean says a complete sentence, don't rewrite it. If he says a fragment, write a complete sentence.

1. **Mandy:** Did you go to the baseball game or to the movies last Saturday?

    Sean: Baseball game.

    _____

2. **Mandy:** Was it a good game?

    Sean: Pretty good.

    _____

3. **Mandy:** Are you going to the game next Saturday?

    Sean: I wouldn't miss it.

    _____

4. **Mandy:** Whom are we playing?

    Sean: Blazers.

    _____

5. **Mandy:** I'd like to go to the game with you.

    Sean: That's a great idea.

    _____

6. **Mandy:** Should I meet you at the ticket office or the bus stop?

    Sean: Ticket office.

    _____

Name _____

Lesson 41

If an item is a fragment, rewrite it as a sentence. If it is a sentence, write correct.

1. Over the mountains.

_____

2. I plan to spend the summer swimming and riding my scooter.

_____

3. Bright stars filled the sky.

_____

4. A large piece of cake.

_____

5. An unusual place.

_____

6. Tadpoles live in our pond.

_____

7. Once a week.

_____

8. Please call when you have time.

_____

Name _____

Lesson 42

Circle the subject and underline the predicate.

1. Paulo plays tennis.

2. Paulo and Steve play tennis often.

3. Paulo and his friends play tennis in the park.

4. Beth's little sister likes to play video games.

5. The angry crowd marched to the state capitol.

6. Some people in the crowd shouted and jeered.

7. The leading race car crashed into a wall.

8. Uncle Fred and Aunt Colleen came for a visit last week.

9. The children and their parents applauded the smiling principal.

10. Dennis, Harry, and Kyle decided to form a ska band.

Name _____

Lesson 43

Circle the subject and underline the predicate in each sentence.

1. Sylvia created her own Web page.

2. My cousin Sylvia created her own Web page as a class project.

3. Ms. Colson teaches geometry and algebra.

4. The New York Yankees won the World Series in 2000.

5. A large red truck roared past us on the narrow road.

6. This unusual painting shows seven different views of the Japanese mountain.

7. Our French class wrote letters to students in Paris.

8. The raging floodwaters reached the second floor of our house.

9. Five happy puppies frolicked and tumbled in the grass.

10. Everybody in the group agreed to donate time to the project.

Name _____

Lesson 44

> • A **noun** is a word that names a person,
> place, thing, idea, or feeling.

Circle the words that can be nouns. Cross out the words that do not name people, places, things, ideas, or feelings.

1. sadly

2. Luke

3. lonely

4. house

5. Kansas

6. Supreme Court

7. tree

8. laugh

45

Name _____

Lesson 45

> • A **common** noun is a word that names *any* person, place, thing, idea, or feeling.
>
> • A **proper** noun names a *particular* person, place, thing, idea, or feeling. Proper nouns always begin with a capital letter.

Write common if a word is a common noun and proper if it is a proper noun.

1. Paula _____

2. shovel _____

3. Detroit _____

4. water _____

5. saddle _____

6. cave _____

7. events _____

8. Abigail _____

9. bridge _____

10. Statue of Liberty _____

11. sister _____

12. Iran _____

Name _____

Lesson 46

> • A **singular** noun names one person, place, thing, idea, or feeling.
>
> • A **plural** noun names more than one.
>
> • Most nouns are made plural by adding **s.**
>
> • Nouns that end with **s, z, ch, sh,** and **x** are made plural by adding **es.**

A. If the noun names one person, place, thing, idea, or feeling, write singular. If it names more than one, write plural.

1. rabbits   _____

2. coat   _____

3. cabbage   _____

4. bushes   _____

5. foxes   _____

B. Write the plural of each noun.

1. bus   _____

2. trumpet   _____

3. kiss   _____

4. church   _____

5. friend   _____

47

Lesson 47

> - Nouns that end with a consonant followed by **y** are made plural by changing the **y** to **i** and adding **es.**
> - Nouns that end with a vowel followed by **y** are made plural by adding **s.**
> - Nouns that end with **f** are made plural by changing the **f** to **v** and adding **es.**

Write the plural of each noun.

1. leaf   _____

2. city   _____

3. day   _____

4. country   _____

5. self   _____

6. turkey   _____

7. loaf   _____

8. thief   _____

9. play   _____

Name _____

Lesson 48

- Some nouns have **irregular** plural forms.
- You can't predict how to make the plural form of an irregular noun. Sometimes you have to check its spelling in a dictionary.

Write the plural of each noun. Use your dictionary.

1. **medium** _____

2. **oasis** _____

3. **child** _____

4. **foot** _____

5. **series** _____

6. **mouse** _____

7. **sheep** _____

8. **woman** _____

> • **Possessive** nouns tell who or what owns or has something.
> • Most singular nouns are made possessive by adding an apostrophe (') and **s**.
> • Most plural nouns ending in **s** are made possessive by adding an apostrophe (').

A. Write S if the noun is singular and P if it is plural. Then write the possessive form.

	Singular/Plural	Possessive
1. Dana	_____	_____
2. babies	_____	_____
3. wolves	_____	_____
4. Lois	_____	_____

B. Write the plural of each noun.

1. box	_____	5. goose	_____
2. calf	_____	6. bench	_____
3. key	_____	7. team	_____
4. wheat	_____	8. cherry	_____

Name _____

Lesson 50

Write the singular and plural possessive.

	Singular Possessive	**Plural Possessive**
1. **tax**	_____	_____
2. **elf**	_____	_____
3. **dish**	_____	_____
4. **journey**	_____	_____
5. **desk**	_____	_____
6. **candy**	_____	_____
7. **waltz**	_____	_____
8. **home**	_____	_____

51

Name _____

> • **Pronouns** are words that take the place of nouns.
> • **Personal pronouns** refer to people or things.
> • Here are some personal pronouns: **I, me, you, he, him, she, her, it, we, us, they, them.**

Circle the pronouns in each sentence.

1. I like to go to movies.

2. The firefighter praised us for acting quickly.

3. Did they give it to him or to her?

4. Please tell me a story.

5. He called them early in the morning.

6. She and Shaunna belong to a book club.

7. Where is he staying?

8. Can we go with you to the zoo?

Name _____

Lesson 52

> • **Possessive pronouns** are words that tell who or what owns something.
>
> • Possessive pronouns can replace possessive nouns.
>
> • Possessive pronouns **aren't** written with apostrophes.
>
> • Here are some possessive pronouns: **my, mine, your, yours, her, hers, his, its, our, ours, their, theirs.**

Rewrite the sentences. Use possessive pronouns.

1. Laura's family is moving to Fairbanks.

   _____

2. Is this Ken's bike helmet, or is it Delia's?

   _____

3. That book belongs to me.

   _____

4. Rugby's rules are hard to understand.

   _____

5. Paula's house is on the same street as Mel's and Brad's.

   _____

6. Dolores's hobby is bird watching.

   _____

Name _____

> - The word that a pronoun refers to is called an **antecedent**.
> - **Antecedent** means "a word that goes before."
> - When you write pronouns, make sure they refer clearly to their antecedents.

If an item has a clear pronoun and antecedent, underline the pronoun and circle its antecedent. If a pronoun doesn't have a clear antecedent, rewrite the item to make it clear.

1. Phil went to the station with Joe. He caught the last train.

_____

2. Mike bought new sneakers. They are orange.

_____

3. Mike bought new sneakers for his brother. He likes orange.

_____

4. Kent invited Nancy to join the chess club. She was thrilled!

_____

5. Sheila told Patrick that she will take calculus next year.

_____

6. Stan is interested in physics. It is a difficult subject.

_____

Name _____

Lesson 54

> - Every sentence has a **verb.**
> - Some verbs express the **action of a sentence.**
> - Verbs can express physical actions: **walk, laugh, look.** They can also express mental actions: **think, plan, forget.**
> - The words **has, have,** and **had** can be action verbs. They can be used alone or with other verbs.

A. Underline the verb in each sentence.

1. Tom remembered the appointment.

2. Tom has remembered the appointment.

3. Tom had an appointment.

4. Elephants live in India.

5. Elephants have trunks.

6. Inez has arrived in Chicago.

B. Write sentences for each verb.

1. **march** _____

_____

2. **have worn** _____

_____

3. **memorize** _____

_____

4. **has forgotten** _____

_____

5. **disappear** _____

_____

55

Lesson 55

- **Linking verbs** are words that connect words in the subject with words in the predicate in order to complete the meaning of a sentence.
- Here are some common linking verbs: **am, be, is, are, was, were, become.**

A. Underline the linking verb in each sentence.

1. The house is quiet.

2. The morning was hot and steamy.

3. The congressman became angry.

4. All the buses were empty.

5. My two grandmothers are friends.

6. I am late.

B. Write sentences for each linking verb.

1. **to be** _____

   _____

2. **were** _____

   _____

3. **become** _____

   _____

4. **am** _____

   _____

5. **was** _____

   _____

Name _____

Lesson 56

> - Verbs tell when the action in a sentence takes place.
> - The name for the form of a verb that tells the time of the action is **tense.**
> - **Present-tense** verbs express actions that happen now or that happen regularly. Present-tense verbs can also express things that are true most of the time.
> - **Plural** subjects use the base form of present-tense verbs. Base forms of verbs don't have added endings.
> - The subjects **I** and **you** also use the base form.
> - **Singular** subjects usually add **s** or **es** to the base form.

Write the correct present-tense form of the verb to finish the sentence.

1. **jump**   She _____.

2. **run**   Frank and his dog _____.

3. **learn**   The students _____ quickly.

4. **like**   Ivan _____ pizza and ice cream.

5. **act**   Billy and I _____ in every play.

6. **seem**   You _____ to be unhappy today.

7. **teach**   Mr. Bauer _____ at Central High.

8. **win**   I hope Jason _____ the award.

9. **sound**   The alarms _____ every time we walk in the door.

Lesson 57

Name _____

> - **Past-tense** verbs express actions that have already happened.
> - Past-tense verbs are usually formed by adding **d** or **ed** to the base verb.
> - The form of past-tense verbs is the same for both singular and plural subjects.

A. Write the past-tense form of the verb to finish the sentence.

1. **mow**   Jamael _____ yards all last summer.

2. **wait**   Betsy _____ twenty minutes for Howard.

3. **explore** The tourists _____ the mission ruins.

4. **watch**   I _____ in horror as the wall tumbled.

5. **help**   Kyle _____ his grandmother clean her attic.

B. For each item, circle the verb. Write present or past to show its tense.

                                                                    Tense

1. Gordon erased the first paragraph of his essay.   _____

2. Do you object to the plan?   _____

3. Jeanne boasted about her new computer.   _____

4. Leslie talks too much!   _____

5. Suzi smiles easily.   _____

Name _____

Lesson 58

> - **Future-tense** verbs express actions that will happen in the future.
> - The future tense is formed by using a **helping verb.**
> - For most verbs, use the helping verb **will** to form the present tense.
> - When the subject of a sentence is **I** or **we,** you can use the helping verb **shall** instead of **will.**

A. Write the future-tense form of the verb to finish the sentence. Remember to write the helping verb.

1. **perform**   I _____ my magic show next Sunday night.

2. **begin**   The show _____ at 8:00.

3. **close**   The theater doors _____ at 8:05.

4. **amaze**   The last trick I do _____ you!

B. For each item, circle the verb. Write present, past, or future to show its tense.

                                                   Tense

1. We shall attend your graduation ceremony.   _____

2. I learned a lot in computer camp last summer.   _____

3. Dan interviewed three people for the job.   _____

4. Piper writes advertisements.   _____

5. Oscar will compose a song for our party.   _____

59

Name _____

Lesson 59

If the verb tenses in a sentence aren't consistent, rewrite the sentence to make them consistent. If the tenses are consistent, don't rewrite the sentence.

1. Mustafa jumps up and stomped out of class.

   _____

   _____

2. The band played loudly and marches badly.

   _____

   _____

3. Mr. Drummond will speak to our group, then he will take questions.

   _____

   _____

4. The boss summons Wayne to the office and yelled at him.

   _____

   _____

5. Chelsea selected the colors and paints her house.

   _____

   _____

Name _____

Lesson 60

> ¹Gabe stared down from his apartment window. ²He sees his friends, Rafe and Lucky, on the street below. ³Rafe wears a top hat. ⁴Lucky wore a red cape. ⁵Lucky tripped. ⁶He grabs a garbage can. ⁷Gabe laughed out loud. ⁸Rafe and Lucky look up at Gabe. ⁹Rafe smiled. ¹⁰He bows deeply to Gabe.

Rewrite only the sentences in the passage that use present-tense verbs. Change the verbs to past tense.

_____

_____

_____

_____

_____

_____

_____

_____

Name _____

Lesson 61

- **Adjectives** are words that describe nouns or pronouns.
- Adjectives answer the questions **what kind**? **how many**? or **which one**?
- More than one adjective may be used to describe a noun or pronoun.

A. For each item, underline the adjective and circle the word the adjective describes. Remember, more than one adjective can be used to describe the same word.

1. We grow pink petunias.

2. Old wooden houses are being rebuilt.

3. Gary collects rare gold coins.

4. Holly found seventeen shiny pennies.

5. Gino drives fast Italian cars.

6. I don't like chocolate yogurt.

7. Debra won't work with silly or lazy people.

B. Write N above the nouns, P above the pronouns, V above the verbs, and A above the adjectives.

1. Our two families quarreled.

2. Forecasters predict many hot, dry autumns.

3. They arranged wonderful parties.

4. My hometown is beautiful Dayton, Ohio.

Name

Lesson 62

- The words **a, an,** and **the** are special adjectives called articles.
- The articles **a** and **an** describe a **general** group of nouns or pronouns.
- The article **the** refers to a **specific** noun or pronoun.
- In general, use **a** before words that begin with consonants. Use **an** before words that begin with vowels.
- Here are some exceptions: **a union, a university, an hour, an honor, an Xray, an F, a European.**

Underline the correct article and circle the word it refers to.

1. Mom's planning to join (a, an) union.

2. Do you know (a, an, the) address where Bailey is staying?

3. I need (a, an) poster to hide the hole in my wall.

4. Gomez plans to attend (a, an, the) college that his dad attended.

5. I saw (a, an) alligator when I was on vacation.

6. Blyth was upset when she received (a, an) F.

7. Can you show me (a, an, the) Xray of my arm?

63

Name _____

Lesson 63

> • **Demonstrative adjectives** describe nouns by answering the questions **which one**? or **which ones**?
>
> • Here are the demonstrative adjectives: **this, that, these,** and **those.**
>
> • **This** and **that** describe singular nouns.
>
> • **These** and **those** describe plural nouns.
>
> • **Never** use the words **here** and **there** with demonstrative adjectives.

A. Underline the correct demonstrative adjective and circle the noun it describes.

1. (These, These here) radios don't work very well.

2. Tomás found (this, these) necklace in the bushes.

3. (This, These) pictures are not very interesting.

4. Where should I put (that, that there) cake?

5. I think my father sold (that, those) books.

6. Julie and Andee own (this, those) store.

B. Write N above the nouns, P above the pronouns, V above the verbs, and A above the adjectives.

1. The new minister preached a long sermon.

2. Those noisy neighbors moved.

3. Cole is the most honest young man I know.

4. That battlefield is a national historic site.

Name _____

Lesson 64

- **Comparative** adjectives compare one noun or pronoun with another.
- To form comparatives of most short adjectives, add the ending **er**.
- To form comparatives of longer adjectives, use the word **more**.
- **Superlative** adjectives compare one noun or pronoun with several others.
- To form superlatives of most short adjectives, add the ending **est**.
- To form superlatives of longer adjectives, use the word **most**.

Write the comparatives and superlatives of each adjective.

		Comparative	Superlative
1.	famous	_____	_____
2.	rich	_____	_____
3.	delicious	_____	_____
4.	slow	_____	_____

B. Write two sentences for each adjective. In the first sentence, use the comparative. In the second sentence, use the superlative.

A. beautiful

1. _____

2. _____

B. young

3. _____

4. _____

65

Name _____

Lesson 65

- Comparatives and superlatives of some adjectives are **irregular.** This means they're not formed by adding **er** or **est** or by using the words **more** or **most.**

- Here are some common adjectives that have irregular comparatives and superlatives:

bad	. . . . worse	/	worst
good	. . . . better	/	best
little	. . . . less	/	least

To finish the sentences, write comparatives and superlatives of the underlined adjective.

A. This year, our team is <u>bad.</u>

1. It's _____ than last year's team.

2. It's the _____ team we've ever had.

B. Neil is a <u>good</u> student.

3. He's a _____ student than Josh is.

4. He's probably the _____ student in our school.

C. This job requires <u>little</u> skill.

5. It requires _____ skill than my other job.

6. In fact, it requires the _____ skill of any job I've ever had.

Name _____

Lesson 66

- **Adverbs** are words that tell more about other parts of speech, especially verbs.
- Adverbs tell **how**? **when**? or **where**? an action is done.
- Many adverbs are formed by adding **ly** to adjectives.

Underline the adverbs and circle the verbs they tell more about.

1. The explorers traveled south for ten miles.

2. I agree reluctantly to your demands.

3. George left hurriedly.

4. Customers return often to our restaurant.

5. Homer lives downstairs from his brother.

6. Please come today.

Name _____

Lesson 67

- You can change some adjectives into adverbs by adding **ly** to the adjective.

    –The word **clever** is an adjective.

    –The word **cleverly** is an adverb.

- Remember:

    –**Adverbs** usually tell about verbs and answer **where**? **when**? or **how**?

    –**Adjectives** describe nouns or pronouns and answer **what kind**? **how many**? or **which one**?

Complete each sentence correctly with an adverb or adjective.

1. **beautiful**   A. The group performed _____.

     B. It was a _____ performance.

2. **slow**   A. She is a _____ worker.

     B. She works _____.

3. **soft**   A. Darla stroked the _____ kitten.

     B. Darla spoke _____.

4. **complete**   A. The movie was a _____ waste.

     B. The movie _____ fooled me.

5. **neat**   A. Nancy is a _____ dresser.

     B. Nancy dresses _____.

Name _____

Lesson 68

> • **Prepositions** are words that relate nouns or pronouns to other words in a sentence.
>
> • Here are some common prepositions: **about, after, around, at, before, behind, between, by, for, from, in, near, of, off, over, to, through, under.**
>
> • A preposition may be more than one word.
>
> • Here are some prepositions that are more than one word: **according to, aside from, because of, except for, in front of, instead of, in place of, next to.**

Underline the propositions and circle the words to which the prepositions relate.

1. Do you have any books by J. K. Rowling?

2. Margaret volunteered in place of Megan.

3. The papers are under the printer.

4. The clock is above the door.

5. Everybody went except for Winston.

6. Your bus stop is near the firehouse.

7. The rain blew through the open window.

8. The disturbance was at the station.

Name _____

Lesson 69

- A **prepositional phrase** is a group of words that begins with a preposition and ends with a noun or pronoun.
- The noun or pronoun in a prepositional phrase is called the **object of the preposition.**

A. Write the prepositional phrase. In the phrase that you write, underline the preposition and circle the object of the preposition.

1. The driver of the car stopped suddenly.

   _____

2. Cindy planted tomatoes behind her house.

   _____

3. A dozen birds landed on the fence.

   _____

4. After the show, let's have ice cream.

   _____

B. Write N above nouns, P above pronouns, V above verbs, A above adjectives, AD above adverbs, and PR above prepositions.

1. Sam walked slowly into the museum.

2. Ivy put the rusty trashcan near the back door.

3. The rally was cancelled because of rain.

Name _____

Lesson 70

> - **Conjunctions** are words that connect parts of a sentence.
> - Here are some common conjunctions: **and, but, nor, or.**
> - Sometimes conjunctions are more than one word.
>   - Here are some conjunction with more than one word: **either . . . or, neither . . . nor, both . . . and, not only . . . but also.**

Underline the conjunctions. Circle the two parts of the sentence they join.

1. Chris watches but doesn't play rugby.

2. Karen and her father enjoy archery.

3. Do you want potato chips or pretzels?

4. Neither the senator nor the representative voted for the bill.

5. Either Ms. Bolton or Ms. Hernandez will be the class sponsor.

6. You can get involved or do nothing.

7. The decision affected not only students but also teachers.

Name _____

Lesson 71

Write N above nouns, P above pronouns, V above verbs, A above adjectives, AD above adverbs, PR above prepositions, and C above conjunctions.

1. Grant and Anne sang five funny songs.

2. Albert slept peacefully under the old oak tree.

3. You won, but I played a better game.

4. Golden eagles often fly and hunt near our lodge.

5. Is Elise a poet or a painter?

6. Neither Mexico nor Korea sent a representative to the meeting in Sweden.

7. These new shoes hurt my feet badly.

Name _____

Lesson 72

> - The main word in a subject is a **noun** or **pronoun.**
> - The main word in a predicate is a **verb.**
> - The main word in the subject must **agree in number** with the main verb in the predicate. This means:
>   —If the main noun or pronoun is **singular,** the verb has to be **singular.**
>   —If the main noun or pronoun is **plural,** the verb has to be **plural.**

Circle the main word in the subject. Write S on the blank if the subject is singular, P if it is plural. Underline the verb that agrees in number with the subject.

1. _____   Space travel (interests, interest) me.

2. _____   Betty and Sara (shares, share) a birthday.

3. _____   (Does, Do) tangerines grow on trees?

4. _____   This snake's fangs (contains, contain) some poison.

5. _____   The birds' nest (sits, sit) on the tree branch.

6. _____   Lilacs only (blooms, bloom) in the early spring.

Name _____

> • **Compound subjects** are made up of two or more parts that have the same predicate.
>
> • The parts of a compound subject are joined by **conjunctions.**
>
> • Compound subjects joined by **and** or **both . . . and,** use **plural** main verbs.
>
> • Compound subjects joined by **or, either . . . or,** or **neither . . . nor** use main verbs that agree with the main noun or pronoun closest to the verb.

Underline the main words in the compound subject, then underline the verb twice that agrees in number with the subject. If a subject uses or, either . . . or or neither . . . nor, circle the word in the subject that must agree with the verb.

1. Either the twins or Grady (appears, appear) in every assembly.

2. Cardinals and robins (lives, live) in this state.

3. Neither the buses nor the train (runs, run) on time.

4. Both the cook and her assistants (bakes, bake) the bread.

5. Mr. Wells or his neighbors (mows, mow) the empty lot.

Name _____

Lesson 74

> • **Compound predicates** are made up of two or more parts that have the same subject.
>
> • The main words in compound predicates are **verbs**.
>
> • The parts of a compound predicate are joined by **conjunctions**.
>
> • Compound predicates always **agree in number** with the subject.

Circle the main word in the subject and underline the verbs that agree in number with the subject.

1. My mother (sings, sing) and (dances, dance).

2. Tracey (sweeps, sweep) or (mops, mop) her floors every day.

3. Postal workers (sorts, sort) and (delivers, deliver) thousands of letters each day.

4. Martin either (hikes, hike) or (bikes, bike) in the fall.

5. Sally (reads, read) and (studies, study) novels.

Name _____

Lesson 75

> • If a sentence contains **a series of three or more items** that are joined by a conjunction, commas are used to separate the items so that the meaning of the sentence is clear.
>
> • If a sentence contains only two items, it **doesn't** use a comma.
>
> • When separating a series of more than two items, **place a comma before the conjunction.**
>
> • The items separated by commas may either be **words** or **groups of words,** such as prepositional phrases.

Rewrite each sentence that needs commas to separate items. If a sentence doesn't need commas, write correct.

1. Glenda is beautiful rich and famous.

   _____

2. I told you to water the plants check the mail and turn off the lights.

   _____

3. Does Greene's sell CD players DVD players or TV sets?

   _____

4. Mary sat in the shade and under an umbrella.

   _____

5. The trail leads over the hill near the woods and into the town.

   _____

6. Please notify David and Rocky about the time change.

   _____

Name _____

Lesson 76

> • When a sentence begins with certain introductory words, such as **yes, no,** or **well,** use a comma to separate the word from the rest of the sentence.
>
> • When a sentence **addresses someone directly by name,** use a comma or commas to separate the name from the rest of the sentence.
>
> • If a sentence is just about someone, **don't** use commas to separate the name from the sentence.

Rewrite the sentences and put commas where they belong. Some sentences may need more than one comma. If a sentence doesn't need commas, write correct.

1. Mr. Morris I believe the answer in the book is wrong.

   _____

2. Mr. Morris checked the answer in the book.

   _____

3. Well I can't understand why this phone doesn't work.

   _____

4. No you can't swim in the lake Michael.

   _____

5. Linda left most of her work undone.

   _____

6. Matt is angry Cathy because you hurt his feelings.

   _____

Lesson 77

Name _____

> - If a date has a month, day, and year, use a comma to separate the numbers of the day from the year.
> - Don't use a comma if the date has only the month and year.
> - Use a comma to separate the names of cities and the names of states or countries.
> - In an address, if the city name is used after a street name, use a comma to separate the street from the city.
> - In an address, don't use a comma after the state name if it is followed by a ZIP code.

Rewrite the sentences with dates or addresses that need commas or that use commas incorrectly. Some sentences may need more than one comma. If the date or address in a sentence is correct, write correct.

1. I met Julie on January 6, 2001.

    _____

2. You can write to me at 24 Park Lane Benton Kentucky 42025.

    _____

3. The *Titanic* sank in April, 1912.

    _____

4. That company has its headquarters in Casper Wyoming.

    _____

5. The plane was headed for London England.

    _____

Name _____

Lesson 78

Rewrite the sentences that need commas. Add commas where they're needed. Some sentences may need more than one comma. If a sentence doesn't need commas, write correct.

1. The streets were full of bicycles taxis trucks and buses.

_____

2. Morgan has moved to 3907 Sunnydale Avenue, Austin, Texas 78712.

_____

3. No that's absolutely not true Charlie.

_____

4. The map led us around the barn down the path and over the fence.

_____

5. My favorite state capital is Richmond Virginia.

_____

6. Tony's great-grandfather came to the United States in June 1901.

_____

7. Well what should we do now?

_____

8. I'm sure Rosalind that the memorial is in Atlanta Georgia.

_____

Name —————————————————

Lesson 79

Rewrite each pair of sentences as a combined sentence.

1. The TV series is a police drama. It is realistic.

   _____

2. Wolfgang is rambunctious. He is a puppy.

   _____

3. Alonzo and Jerrod are volunteers. They are cheerful.

   _____

4. Denise is a golfer. She is a professional.

   _____

5. Dr. Higgins is a teacher. He is strict.

   _____

Name _____

Lesson 80

Use the conjunctions to rewrite each pair of sentences as a combined sentence.

1. **and**   The morning was cold. It was rainy.

_____

2. **or**   Ernie may visit Alabama. He may visit Mississippi.

_____

3. **but**   The ride was short. It was fun.

_____

4. **or**   The Burts may buy a car. They may buy a SUV.

_____

5. **and**   Liz wore a blue sweater. She wore a plaid skirt.

_____

6. **but**   Steve is shy. He is nice.

_____

Lesson 81

> • **Compound sentences** are two complete sentences that are linked with the conjunctions **and, but,** or **or.**
>
> • In a compound sentence, **use a comma** before the conjunction.

Rewrite the pairs of sentences as compound sentences. Use the conjunctions. Remember to put commas where they're needed.

1. **and**   Amy opened the window. Dust blew into her room.

   _____

2. **or**   We'll talk to the principal. We'll go to the school board meeting.

   _____

3. **and**   Katrina began to play. The crowd became silent

   _____

4. **but**   Ricky had tickets. He couldn't get into the stadium.

   _____

5. **or**   Libby can leave now. She can wait for us.

   _____

6. **but**   Grandpop is old. He is very fast.

   _____

Name _____

Lesson 82

A. If an item is a compound sentence, write compound. If it isn't a compound sentence, write no.

1. _____   Is the tent in the front yard or in the garage?

2. _____   I want to have a party, but I can't invite everyone.

3. _____   Eli wants to play hockey, and he wants to be a goalie.

4. _____   The storm was powerful but brief.

5. _____   The horse was breathing hard and sweating.

B. Use the conjunctions to rewrite each pair of sentences as a compound sentence. Put commas where they're needed.

1. **or**   Buck said he would clean his room. He would study.

_____

2. **but**   The plane left on time. It arrived an hour late.

_____

3. **and**   Valerie was embarrassed. She wanted to hide her face.

_____

4. **but**   Stu found the safe. He didn't know the combination.

_____

Name _____

> • **Contractions** are words that are made by combining two words and leaving out one or more letters.
>
> • Use **apostrophes** in contractions to show where letters have been left out.

Common Contractions

aren't	/	are not	isn't	/	is not
doesn't	/	does not	she'll	/	she will
didn't	/	did not	she's	/	she has, she is
hasn't	/	has not	they'll	/	they will
here's	/	here is	they've	/	they have
he'll	/	he will	we'll	/	we will
he's	/	he has, he is	we're	/	we are
I'm	/	I am	you'll	/	you will

A. Write the two words that make each contraction.

1. _____ You'll need to bring lunch.

2. _____ Congress hasn't passed that bill.

3. _____ My dog didn't obey the command.

4. _____ Barney isn't sure that he can go with us.

5. _____ Look, here's the map we need.

B. For each item, underline the two words that can make a contraction. Write the contractions on the blanks.

1. _____ I am going to Hillary's birthday party!

2. _____ She has invited ten people.

3. _____ She will give us ice cream and cake.

4. _____ After we eat, we will play games.

5. _____ Her brother says he is going to do magic tricks.

Name _____

Lesson 84

Homophones	Contractions
1. there, their	they're
2. theirs	there's
3. your	you're
4. its	it's

If a sentence is correct, write correct. If a sentence uses a homophone instead of the correct contraction, rewrite it so that it uses two words that make the correct contraction.

[1]Kirsten and her family are moving. [2]Their buying an old Victorian house. [3]Its the biggest house on the block. [4]Your not going to believe how many rooms it has. [5]It has four floors. [6]Theirs a kitchen on each floor. [7]Kirsten says there planning to turn the house into a bed-and-breakfast.

1. _____

2. _____

3. _____

4. _____

5. _____

6. _____

7. _____

85

Name _____

Lesson 85

Fill in the circle next to the word that is an antonym for the underlined word.

1. Colby's long journey across the mountains left him feeling <u>weary</u>.

   ○ tired   ○ worried   ○ rested

2. If we're going to win the election, we must <u>unite</u> our supporters.

   ○ divide   ○ organize   ○ educate

3. The evil prince was especially <u>cruel</u> to the poor.

   ○ mean   ○ kind   ○ royal

4. Be <u>cautious</u> when you use these chemicals, or they'll explode.

   ○ careful   ○ careless   ○ thoughtful

5. I can never understand Mr. Kelly's <u>complicated</u> instructions.

   ○ simple   ○ difficult   ○ loud

6. This poem is by an <u>obscure</u> poet that few people know about.

   ○ unknown   ○ famous   ○ bad

7. Ari took a <u>temporary</u> job until he could find a job he really wants.

   ○ boring   ○ short   ○ permanent

8. That silly duck hat makes you look <u>ridiculous</u>.

   ○ funny   ○ large   ○ sensible

9. Brian is so <u>arrogant</u> he thinks he's the only person who knows anything.

   ○ humble   ○ rude   ○ lonely

230   BLM 85

Name _____

Lesson 86

Fill in the circle next to the word that is a synonym for the underlined word.

1. Dan likes to <u>stroll</u> slowly through the park each evening.

   ○ run   ○ look   ○ amble

2. Losing what should have been an easy game <u>humiliated</u> the team.

   ○ embarrassed   ○ surprised   ○ delighted

3. You stood by me before, so I know you are <u>reliable</u>.

   ○ beautiful   ○ trustworthy   ○ tricky

4. The discovery is so wonderful, it will <u>astonish</u> you.

   ○ amaze   ○ upset   ○ confuse

5. The tornado hit <u>abruptly</u>, without any warning at all.

   ○ slowly   ○ suddenly   ○ helplessly

6. Tommy is feeling <u>glum</u> because he lost his dog.

   ○ sad   ○ sleepy   ○ angry

7. If you do this favor for me, you'll have my lifelong <u>gratitude</u>.

   ○ insurance   ○ confidence   ○ thanks

8. It looks as if our fundraiser will <u>surpass</u> even our highest goals.

   ○ exceed   ○ fail   ○ match

87

Lesson 87

A. Use the information in each passage to figure out the meaning of the underlined word. Fill in the circle next to the antonym for the underlined word. Use your dictionary to help.

1. The sisters are very different. Jenna is shy, and Rebecca is <u>extroverted</u>.

   ○ outgoing   ○ tall   ○ timid

2. The editor wanted to <u>delete</u> the story from the paper. The publisher wanted it to stay in.

   ○ keep   ○ remove   ○ copy

3. The first speech was <u>tedious</u>. The second one, however, was lively.

   ○ interesting   ○ dull   ○ short

B. Fill in the circle next to the synonym for the underlined word. Use your dictionary to help.

1. The sisters are very different. Jenna is shy, and Rebecca is <u>extroverted</u>.

   ○ outgoing   ○ tall   ○ timid

2. The editor wanted to <u>delete</u> the story from the paper. The publisher wanted it to stay in.

   ○ keep   ○ remove   ○ copy

3. The first speech was <u>tedious</u>. The second one, however, was lively.

   ○ interesting   ○ dull   ○ short

Name _____

Lesson 88

Answer the questions about the paragraphs. Use your dictionary.

Paragraph 1

The senator gave her usual **monotonous** speech about spending too much. We'd heard the speech so often, it almost to put us to sleep. I wish she'd find something more interested to talk about.

Questions

1. What part of speech is <u>monotonous</u>? _____

2. What clues in the context help you figure out what <u>monotonous</u> means?

   _____

3. What does <u>monotonous</u> probably mean?

   _____

Paragraph 2

When Harriet is sad, Andrew can always **cajole** her into feeling better. He tells Harriet how pretty she looks, how smart she is, and how much people like being around her.

Questions

1. What part of speech is <u>cajole</u>? _____

2. What clues in the context help you figure out what <u>cajole</u> means?

   _____

3. What does <u>cajole</u> probably mean?

   _____

Name _____

Lesson 89

A. Answer the questions about the paragraph. Use your dictionary.

Paragraph

The king's **impertinence** was unbearable to his people. He insulted them. He called them names. Finally, they told him they would no longer put up with his ill-mannered behavior.

Questions

1. What part of speech is <u>impertinence</u>? _____

2. What clues in the context help you figure out what <u>impertinence</u> means?

   _____

3. What does <u>impertinence</u> probably mean?

   _____

B. Rewrite each sentence. Replace the underlined words with monotonous, cajole, or impertinence.

1. Your <u>rudeness</u> hurts my feelings.

   _____

2. That radio station plays <u>boring</u> music.

   _____

3. Amos tried to <u>coax</u> Martha to enter the beauty contest.

   _____

Name _____

Lesson 90

A. Answer the questions about the paragraph. Use your dictionary.

Paragraph

The agents entered the country **covertly.** No one saw them, and no one knew who they were. They were able to sneak into the city without being seen.

Questions

1. What part of speech is <u>covertly</u>? _____

2. What clues in the context help you figure out what <u>covertly</u> means?

_____

3. What does <u>covertly</u> probably mean?

_____

B. Rewrite each sentence. Replace the underlined words with monotonous, cajole, impertinence, or covertly.

1. The shoplifter <u>secretly</u> slipped the CD under his jacket.

_____

2. The waiter's <u>rudeness</u> made us leave the restaurant.

_____

3. Don't tell us that <u>boring</u> story again!

_____

4. Can I <u>coax</u> you into lending me your calculator?

_____

91

Name _____

Lesson 91

> • **Similes** are expressions used in speech and writing to compare things that aren't really alike.
> • Similes always use the words **like** or **as.**

Answer the questions about each simile. Use your dictionary.

Reba's smile is like the sun.

1. What two things are compared? _____

   _____

2. How are they similar? _____

   _____

Beau is as strong as a bull.

3. What two things are similar? _____

   _____

4. How are they similar? _____

   _____

My cousin walks like a duck.

5. What two things are similar? _____

   _____

6. How are they similar? _____

   _____

Name _____

Lesson 92

Answer the questions about each simile. Use your dictionary.

It's like midnight in this room!

1. What two things are compared? _____

   _____

2. How are they similar? _____

   _____

Chandra's laugh is as sweet as honey.

3. What two things are compared? _____

   _____

4. How are they similar? _____

   _____

Deena is a timid as a mouse.

5. What two things are compared? _____

   _____

6. How are they similar? _____

   _____

Name _____

Lesson 93

> • **Metaphors** are another kind of expression used in speech and writing to compare things that aren't really alike.
> • Metaphors **don't** use the words **like** or **as**.

Answer the questions about each metaphor. Use your dictionary.

The tornado was an angry child.

1. What two things are compared? _____

_____

2. How are they similar? _____

_____

Marley is an encyclopedia.

3. What two things are compared? _____

_____

4. How are they similar? _____

_____

Our classroom is a freezer.

5. What two things are compared? _____

_____

6. How are they similar? _____

_____

Name _____

Lesson 94

A. Answer the questions about each metaphor. Use your dictionary.

The Wrestling Wild Man is a mountain!

1. What two things are compared? _____

_____

2. How are they similar? _____

_____

When she dances, Katerina is a feather in the wind.

3. What two things are compared? _____

_____

4. How are they similar? _____

_____

The pond is a mirror.

5. What two things are compared? _____

_____

6. How are they similar? _____

_____

B. Write S next to each simile and M next to each metaphor.

1. _____ Kimba is a swan.

2. _____ Your smile is the sun to me.

3. _____ Pete is as sharp as a tack.

4. _____ My tractor runs like a deer.

Name _____

> • **Personification** is a kind of expression that describes nonliving things as humans.
> • Nonliving things described as humans are **personified**.

Answer the questions about each personification.

As she opened the door, the icy wind slapped Tori in the face.

1. What is being personified? _____

2. How is it personified? _____

_____

The stars winked at me.

3. What is being personified? _____

4. How is it personified? _____

_____

The rosebuds smiled up at us from the garden.

5. What is being personified? _____

6. How is it personified? _____

_____

Name _____

Lesson 96

A. Answer the questions about each personification.

The tree branch grabbed Billy's shirt.

1. What is being personified? _____

2. How is it personified? _____

   _____

The campfire spit sparks at the ranger.

3. What is being personified? _____

4. How is it personified? _____

   _____

B. Fill in the circle next to the kind of figure of speech that is used in the sentence.

1. The moon was as bright as a lantern.
   ○ simile   ○ metaphor   ○ personification

2. Larry is dynamite.
   ○ simile   ○ metaphor   ○ personification

3. I'm a chicken when it comes to rock climbing.
   ○ simile   ○ metaphor   ○ personification

4. The sofa invited me to take a nap.
   ○ simile   ○ metaphor   ○ personification

5. In that shirt, you'll stand out like a sore thumb.
   ○ simile   ○ metaphor   ○ personification

Name _____

Lesson 97

Write what each idiom really means.

1. The school's new gym cost an arm and a leg to build.

   _____

   _____

2. After winning the contest, Alice was walking on air.

   _____

   _____

3. I get cold feet every time I have to talk to the class.

   _____

   _____

4. After spilling the soup in my lap, the waiter said my lunch was on the house.

   _____

   _____

5. I hope you'll drop me a line after you move.

   _____

   _____

Name _____

Lesson 98

Write what each idiom really means.

1. Money just burns a hole in Brent's pocket.

   _____

   _____

2. It's raining cats and dogs.

   _____

   _____

3. Cassie and Polly stole the show with their dancing.

   _____

   _____

4. Jimmy looks down in the dumps.

   _____

   _____

B. Fill in the circle next to the kind of figure of speech that is used in the sentence.

1. The dish washer grumbled and groaned, but it washed the big load of dishes.

   ○ simile   ○ metaphor   ○ personification

2. My computer is a dinosaur.

   ○ simile   ○ metaphor   ○ personification

3. I'm as hungry as a bear.

   ○ simile   ○ metaphor   ○ personification

4. The blowing trash danced and skipped down the street.

   ○ simile   ○ metaphor   ○ personification

Name _____

Lesson 99

- **Semicolons (;)** are used in writing to show longer pauses than commas.
- **Semicolons** can be used to join two complete thoughts in compound sentences.
- When semicolons are used in **compound sentences,** they take the place of commas and conjunctions.

Rewrite the sentences. Put semicolons where they belong.

1. I have information about three summer camps I can't tell which one is best.

   _____

   _____

2. Look at that sunset I've never seen anything so beautiful.

   _____

   _____

3. Mr. Garza is a great Spanish teacher he grew up in Mexico.

   _____

   _____

4. E. B. White was a great writer he wrote *Charlotte's Web.*

   _____

   _____

5. Vonda called me yesterday she wanted to go to skating.

   _____

   _____

Name _____

Lesson 100

> • Use **semicolons (;)** to separate parts of
> sentences if one or more of the parts
> already use commas.

Fill in the circles next to the sentences that use semicolons in the correct places.

1. ○ Is United Telephone's main office in Roanoke, Virginia, Jackson, Mississippi, or Waco, Texas?

2. ○ Is United Telephone's main office in Roanoke, Virginia; Jackson, Mississippi; or Waco, Texas?

3. ○ You can write your report on *Shiloh*; written by Phyllis Reynolds Naylor; *Julie of the Wolves*; written by Jean Craighead George; or *Island of the Blue Dolphins*; written by Scott O'Dell.

4. ○ You can write your report on *Shiloh*, written by Phyllis Reynolds Naylor; *Julie of the Wolves*, written by Jean Craighead George; or *Island of the Blue Dolphins*, written by Scott O'Dell.

5. ○ We rented costumes, lights, and props; built a set in the park; and made a video to show the class.

6. ○ We rented costumes, lights, and props; built a set in the park, and made a video to show the class.

Name _____

Lesson 101

> - **Colons (:)** direct reader's attention to what a writer wants to highlight.
> - When a sentence contains words and phrases such as **these, the following,** or **as follows,** use colons to introduce **a list of items.**
> - **Don't** use colons to introduce a list of items if the list follows a verb or preposition.

Rewrite only the sentences that don't use colons correctly. You'll put colons in some sentences and take them out of others. If a sentence is correct, write correct.

1. Mom's grocery list contained these items: milk, bread, and juice.

   _____

   _____

2. I send e-mails to: Charlie, Derek, Phoebe, and Kirsten.

   _____

   _____

3. My schedule includes the following classes art, math, science, reading, social studies, and music.

   _____

   _____

4. The sports I like best are hockey, skating, and wrestling.

   _____

   _____

Name _____

Lesson 102

Fill in the circles next to the sentences that use semicolons and colons in the correct places.

1. ○ Please check to see that you have these things: paper, pencil, test booklet, and dictionary.

2. ○ Please check to see that you have these things; paper, pencil, test booklet, and dictionary.

3. ○ Please check to see that you have these things paper, pencil, test booklet, and dictionary.

4. ○ We need to: mop the floors; dust the desk, tables, and shelves; and wash all of the windows.

5. ○ We need to mop the floors; dust the desk, tables, and shelves; and wash all of the windows.

6. ○ We need to mop the floors: dust the desk, tables, and shelves: and wash all of the windows.

7. ○ Zander wants to see you he has a plan for the project.

8. ○ Zander wants to see you: he has a plan for the project.

9. ○ Zander wants to see you; he has a plan for the project.

Lesson 103

- **Quotation marks (" ")** are always used in pairs. They highlight the words that come between them.

- Use quotation marks around the **exact words** that somebody says or writes. The exact words are called a **quotation.**

- Begin quotations with **capital letters.** Put periods **inside** the closing quotation marks.

- If they're part of the quotation, put **question marks** and **exclamation points inside** the closing quotation marks.

- If they're part of the sentence but not the quotation, put **question marks** and **exclamation points outside** the closing quotation marks.

- Use **commas** to set off words such as **he said** or **she asks** from the quotation.

Fill in the circles next to the sentences that use quotation marks and other punctuation marks correctly. Look at the information in the box for help.

1. ○ "Dad said, Take these clothes to the cleaners."

2. ○ Dad said, "Take these clothes to the cleaners."

3. ○ George asked, "Which way to the depot?"

4. ○ George asked "Which way to the depot?"

5. ○ Do you remember who said, "A penny for your thoughts?"

6. ○ Do you remember who said, "A penny for your thoughts"?

Name _____

Lesson 104

> - Sometimes a quotation starts a sentence. Words such as **he says** or **she wrote** come after the quotation.
> - When the quotation starts a sentence, write the opening quotation marks first and use a **capital letter** for the first word.
> - Put a punctuation mark at the end of the quotation and before the closing quotation marks. These punctuation marks can be **commas, periods, question marks,** or **exclamation points.**
> - Put a period after the word at the end of the sentence.

Fill in the circles next to the sentences that use quotation marks and other punctuation marks correctly. Look at the information in the box for help.

1. ○ "Who wants to go get yogurt?" Connie called.

2. ○ "Who wants to go get yogurt" Connie called?

3. ○ "You'll need to work on this after class." Ms. Leone said

4. ○ "You'll need to work on this after class," Ms. Leone said.

5. ○ "I can't believe you said that"! Tony laughed.

6. ○ "I can't believe you said that!" Tony laughed.

7. ○ "Where's the car?" Yoko asked.

8. ○ "Where's the car"? Yoko asked.

Lesson 105

- Sometimes a quotation is split in a sentence. Part of it comes before words such as **he says** or **she called** and part of it comes after.

- When the quotation is split, put quotation marks at the beginning and at the end of each part.

- For the first part, write opening quotation marks and use a capital letter for the first word. Put a comma before the closing quotation marks.

- Put a comma after the words that tell who said the quotation.

- For the second part of the quotation, write opening quotation marks, but **don't** use a capital letter for the first word. Put a period, question mark, or exclamation point before the closing quotation marks.

Fill in the circles next to the sentences that use quotation marks and other punctuation marks correctly. Look at the information in the box for help.

1. ○ "I heard," Mac said. "That Chuck is moving."

2. ○ "I heard," Mac said, "that Chuck is moving."

3. ○ "If you don't hurry." Carolyn called, "we'll be late."

4. ○ "If you don't hurry," Carolyn called, "we'll be late."

5. ○ "Just wait a minute," Donna laughed, "and the weather will change."

6. ○ "Just wait a minute, Donna laughed, and the weather will change."

Name _____

Lesson 106

- **Hyphens (-)** can **link** words.
- Use hyphens to link words when the words come before a noun and work together to describe, or modify the noun: a **well-known** artist, a **hair-raising** accident, a **once-in-a-lifetime** offer.
- **Don't** use hyphens to link words when they come after a noun: the artist is **well known,** the accident was **hair raising.**
- **Don't** use hyphens with adverbs that end in **ly:** a **quickly** written note, a **newly** built store.

Fill in the circles next to the sentences that use hyphens correctly.

1. ○ Maureen gave her new neighbors a **house warming** gift.

2. ○ Maureen gave her new neighbors a **house-warming** gift.

3. ○ He is an **unusually kind** person.

4. ○ He is an **unusually-kind** person.

5. ○ Betsy's story was **bone chilling.**

6. ○ Betsy's story was **bone-chilling.**

7. ○ I saw a **ruby throated** finch yesterday.

8. ○ I saw a **ruby-throated** finch yesterday.

9. ○ Sidney left a **quickly written** note.

10. ○ Sidney left a **quickly-written** note.

Name _____

Lesson 107

Rewrite only the sentences that don't use hyphens correctly. You'll put in some hyphens and take some out. If a sentence is correct, write correct.

1. Warren wore a sky-blue suit and shoes that were snow white.

_____

_____

2. We were caught unprepared by the rapidly-moving storm.

_____

_____

3. Did you see those ruby red slippers?

_____

_____

4. The McCall family's dogs are always well-behaved.

_____

_____

5. Barbara has become a well-known poet.

_____

_____

6. Alex asked for an up or down vote.

_____

_____

7. I stared sadly at the completely-flat tire.

_____

_____

Name _____

Lesson 108

> - **Facts** are statements that can be proved. Facts can be proved with the following:
>   —**statistics,** or numbers
>   —**examples**
> - **Opinions** are personal beliefs or feelings. Opinions **can't** be proved.

Write fact if the statement can be proved. Write opinion if it's just a feeling or belief that can't be proved.

1. _____   Last year, teenagers bought more than 20 million CDs.

2. _____   Most of the CDs teenagers buy are just loud noise.

3. _____   The average CD costs about fifteen dollars.

4. _____   Some CDs cost as much as thirty dollars.

5. _____   No CD is worth thirty dollars!

6. _____   Music on CDs is better than the music on old vinyl records.

7. _____   CDs weren't available thirty years ago.

> There's no better place to live than Charleston, West Virginia. Charleston is the capital of West Virginia. It's the prettiest state capital in the United States. Charleston is located in the Allegheny Mountains. The hiking trails in the Alleghenies are much better than those in the Rockies. The views from the mountains can't be beat. Charleston is also near the Elk and Kanawha rivers. The people in Charleston are the friendliest in the country.

Write fact if the statement can be proved. Write opinion if it's just a feeling or belief that can't be proved.

1. _____ There's no better place to live than Charleston, West Virginia.

2. _____ Charleston is the capital city of West Virginia.

3. _____ It's the prettiest state capital in the United States.

4. _____ Charleston is located in the Allegheny Mountains.

5. _____ The hiking trails in the Alleghenies are much better than those in the Rockies.

6. _____ The views from the mountains can't be beat.

7. _____ Charleston is also near the Elk and Kanawha rivers.

8. _____ The people in Charleston are the friendliest in the country.

Name _____

Lesson 110

> **Time Words and Expressions**
>
> today, tomorrow, yesterday, last month, next year, this morning, ago, once, now, past
>
> **Order Words and Expressions**
>
> after, at first, at last, before, during, finally, first, later, last, next, second, then, third

A. Circle the words in each paragraph that signal time or order.

1. Ana decided to make a cake. The first thing she did was find the flour, eggs, and sugar. The second thing she did was locate the cake pan. The third thing she did was mix the batter. Then she put the cake in the oven. The last thing Ana did was eat the cake.

2. I visited my cousins last month; next week I'll visit my great-grandpop. I hope I can visit Aunt Flo later.

B. Write two paragraphs. In the first, use time words and expressions from the box to signal when something happened. In the second paragraph, use order words and expressions from the box to signal the order in which things happen.

_____

_____

_____

_____

_____

111

Lesson 111

Location Words and Expressions

above, across, around, beside, behind, between, in,
in front of, in back of, inside, near, next to, on,
outside, over, straight ahead, through, under, right,
left, up, down

A. Circle the words in each paragraph that signal location.

1.   Greg walked through the door of his mother's office. She sat behind
her desk, frowning. In front of her on the desk was Greg's report card.

2.   When you enter the woods, walk straight ahead for about a mile.
You'll come to two paths. Take the path on your left. Go between the
two big rocks, and you'll see a stream. Follow it down to the falls. Our
cabin is next to the falls.

**B. Write a paragraph. Use location words and expressions from the box
to signal where something is.**

_____

_____

_____

_____

_____

_____

Name _____

Lesson 112

> **Words and Expressions That Signal Change**
>
> although, but, however, instead, on the other hand, otherwise, rather, yet

A. Circle the words in each paragraph that signal changes.

1.   I told my sister that I'd help her clean the house. Instead, I went to play with my friends. I feel terrible about letting her down. On the other hand, she'd probably do the same to me.

2.   Brenda told me I'd like making pottery, although it's very hard to do. She said that I'd learn fast, however. Rather than argue with her, I said I'd give it a try.

B. Write a paragraph. Use words and expressions from the box to signal change.

_____

_____

_____

_____

_____

_____

_____

_____

113

Name _____

Lesson 113

Words That Signal Cause-and-Effect Relationships

because, so, therefore

Answer the questions about each cause-and-effect relationship.

The boat hit a rock; therefore, it had to be repaired.

1. What happened? _____

2. What caused it to happen? _____

3. What word signals the relationship between what happened and what

   caused it to happen? _____

Ivy twisted her ankle, so she lost the race.

4. What happened? _____

5. What caused it to happen? _____

6. What word signals the relationship between what happened and what

   caused it to happen? _____

Cassidy took a summer job because he wanted to earn money.

7. What happened? _____

8. What caused it to happen? _____

9. What word signals the relationship between what happened and what

   caused it to happen? _____

Name _____

Lesson 114

- A **run-on sentence** is two or more sentences that are combined with conjunctions.
- To correct a run-on sentence, rewrite it as two or more separate sentences.

Rewrite each run-on sentence as two or more separate sentences. Don't use any conjunctions. Remember to start each sentence with a capital letter and end it with a period.

1. We went to the fair and we rode the rides and we had popcorn.

    _____

    _____

    _____

2. Mr. Marcelli made the posters and Tricia decorated the room and Benny took the tickets.

    _____

    _____

    _____

3. The village is more than five hundred years old but it is in the mountains and it is hard to get to but it is beautiful.

    _____

    _____

    _____

Name _____

Lesson 115

Rewrite each run-on sentence as two or more separate sentences. Don't use any conjunctions. Remember to start each sentence with a capital letter and end it with a period.

1. We were surprised to get a package and we tore it open but it was just a video ad from a toothpaste company.

   _____

   _____

   _____

2. Mildred hoped her book would be read by students and she hoped it would be made into a movie but she never thought it would win a prize.

   _____

   _____

   _____

3. Tim had to outline the project and he had to find the camera and he had to take the pictures but he finished everything on time.

   _____

   _____

   _____

Name _____

Lesson 116

In the yard, the boys saw a dog.

Picture A   **Picture B**

Rewrite the sentence so that it tells about Picture A.

_____

_____

_____

Rewrite the sentence so that it tells about Picture B.

_____

_____

_____

Name _____

Lesson 117

The cat saw the mouse.

Picture A

Picture B

Rewrite the sentence so that it tells about Picture A.

_____

_____

_____

Rewrite the sentence so that it tells about Picture B.

_____

_____

_____

Name _____

Lesson 118

The dog chased the puppy.

Picture A   Picture B

Rewrite the sentence so that it tells about Picture A.

_____

_____

_____

Rewrite the sentence so that it tells about Picture B.

_____

_____

_____

Name _____

Lesson 119

Our street has tall buildings and trees.

Picture A   **Picture B**

Rewrite the sentence so that it tells about Picture A.

_____

_____

_____

Rewrite the sentence so that it tells about Picture B.

_____

_____

_____

Name _____

Lesson 120

The store sells old books and newspapers.

Picture A   **Picture B**

Rewrite the sentence so that it tells about picture A.

_____

_____

_____

Rewrite the sentence so that it tells about picture B.

_____

_____

_____